OXFORD WORLD'S CLASSICS

OSCAR WILDE
COMPLETE POETRY

OSCAR WILDE was born in Dublin in 1854. Self-advertised, he became the most notorious of late nineteenth-century aesthetes, renowned for his conversation and wit. He published early poetry, followed by short stories, fairy-tales, and the sensational novel *The Picture of Dorian Gray*. He wrote two sparkling critical dialogues, and achieved public success as a comic playwright, crowned by *The Importance of Being Earnest* in 1895. But in that year the flamboyance of his lifestyle and his friendship with Lord Alfred Douglas led at last to his trial and imprisonment for two years' hard labour, for homosexual offences. After his imprisonment he wrote his most famous poem, *The Ballad of Reading Gaol*. He died in Paris in 1900.

ISOBEL MURRAY, Senior Lecturer in English at Aberdeen University, edited *The Picture of Dorian Gray* in the Oxford English Novels series in 1974, and Wilde's *Complete Shorter Fiction* for Oxford University Press in 1979. She has also edited The Oxford Authors Series, *Writings of Oscar Wilde*, in 1989, and Wilde's *The Soul of Man and Prison Writings* in Oxford World's Classics in 1990.

OXFORD WORLD'S CLASSICS

*For almost 100 years Oxford World's Classics have brought
readers closer to the world's great literature. Now with over 700
titles—from the 4,000-year-old myths of Mesopotamia to the
twentieth century's greatest novels—the series makes available
lesser-known as well as celebrated writing.*

*The pocket-sized hardbacks of the early years contained
introductions by Virginia Woolf, T. S. Eliot, Graham Greene,
and other literary figures which enriched the experience of reading.
Today the series is recognized for its fine scholarship and
reliability in texts that span world literature, drama and poetry,
religion, philosophy and politics. Each edition includes perceptive
commentary and essential background information to meet the
changing needs of readers.*

OXFORD WORLD'S CLASSICS

OSCAR WILDE

Complete Poetry

Edited with an Introduction and Notes by
ISOBEL MURRAY

OXFORD
UNIVERSITY PRESS

OXFORD

UNIVERSITY PRESS

Great Clarendon Street, Oxford OX2 6DP

Oxford University Press is a department of the University of Oxford.
It furthers the University's objective of excellence in research, scholarship,
and education by publishing worldwide in

Oxford New York

Athens Auckland Bangkok Bogotá Buenos Aires Calcutta
Cape Town Chennai Dar es Salaam Delhi Florence Hong Kong Istanbul
Karachi Kuala Lumpur Madrid Melbourne Mexico City Mumbai
Nairobi Paris São Paulo Singapore Taipei Tokyo Toronto Warsaw

with associated companies in Berlin Ibadan

Oxford is a registered trade mark of Oxford University Press
in the UK and in certain other countries

Published in the United States
by Oxford University Press Inc., New York

Editorial material © Isobel Murray 1997

First published as a World's Classics paperback 1997
Reissued as an Oxford World's Classics paperback 1998

British Library Cataloguing in Publication Data

Data available

Library of Congress Cataloging in Publication Data

Wilde, Oscar, 1854–1900.
[Poems]
Complete poetry/Oscar Wilde; edited by Isobel Murray.
p. cm.—(Oxford world's classics)
Includes bibliographical references and index.
I. Murray, Isobel. II. Title. III. Series.
PR5814 1997 821'.8—dc20 96–41420

ISBN 0–19–283526-2

3 5 7 9 10 8 6 4 2

Printed in Great Britain by
Cox & Wyman Ltd.
Reading, Berkshire

Contents

Acknowledgments   viii

Introduction   ix

Chronology   xvii

Note on the Text   xix

Chorus of Cloud–Maidens   I
From Spring Days to Winter   2
Requiescat   3
San Miniato   4
By the Arno   4
Rome Unvisited   5
La Bella Donna Della Mia Mente   7
Chanson   8
The Dole of the King's Daughter   9
Αἴλινον, αἴλινον εἰπέ, τὸ δ' εὖ νικάτω   10
The True Knowledge   11
Θρηνωδία   11
Lotus Leaves   14
A Fragment from the Agamemnon of Aeschylos   17
A Vision   20
Sonnet on Approaching Italy   20
Sonnet Written in Holy Week at Genoa   21
Impression de Voyage   21
The Theatre at Argos   22
Urbs Sacra Æterna   22
The Grave of Keats   23
Sonnet on the Massacre of the Christians in Bulgaria   23
Easter Day   24
Sonnet on Hearing the Dies Iræ Sung in the Sistine Chapel   24
Italia   25
Vita Nuova   25
E Tenebris   26
Quantum Mutata   26
To Milton   27
Ave Maria Plena Gratia   27
Wasted Days   28

The Grave of Shelley	28
Santa Decca	29
Theoretikos	29
Amor Intellectualis	30
At Verona	30
Ravenna	31
Magdalen Walks	40
The Burden of Itys	41
Theocritus: A Villanelle	51
Endymion	52
Charmides	53
Ballade de Marguerite	73
Humanitad	74
Athanasia	87
The New Helen	89
Panthea	92
Phèdre	97
Queen Henrietta Maria	98
Louis Napoleon	98
Madonna Mia	99
Roses and Rue	99
Portia	102
Apologia	102
Quia Multum Amavi	103
Silentium Amoris	104
Her Voice	105
My Voice	106
Γλυκύπικρος ἔρως	106
The Garden of Eros	108
Ave Imperatrix	117
Pan: Double Villanelle	121
Sen Artysty; or, The Artist's Dream	122
Libertatis Sacra Fames	125
Sonnet to Liberty	126
Tædium Vitæ	126
Fabien dei Franchi	127
Serenade	127
Camma	128
Impression du Matin	129
In the Gold Room: A Harmony	130
Impressions: I. Les Silhouettes	130

Impressions: II. La Fuite de la Lune   131
Impression: Le Réveillon   131
Hélas!   132
Impressions: I. Le Jardin   132
               II. La Mer   133
Le Jardin des Tuileries   133
The Harlot's House   134
Fantaisies Décoratives: I. Le Panneau   136
                      II. Les Ballons   137
Under the Balcony   138
To My Wife: With a Copy of My Poems   139
Sonnet on the Sale by Auction of Keats' Love Letters   139
The New Remorse   140
Canzonet   140
With a Copy of 'A House of Pomegranates'   141
Symphony in Yellow   141
In the Forest   142
The Sphinx   142
The Ballad of Reading Gaol   152

Appendix   173
Notes   175
Further Reading   207
Index of Titles and First Lines   208

Acknowledgements

GRATEFUL thanks are due to Professor Bobby Fong, as indicated in the Note on the Text. In Aberdeen, particular thanks go to Dominic Mitchell, whose contribution to this volume has been invaluable. Also to Sabine Shand, for translating German criticism. Graeme Roberts encouraged me to apply for some substitute teaching so as to meet contract deadlines, and Aberdeen University's Queen Mother Library has been as helpful as ever. I am indebted to the Aberdeen University Research Committee for a grant for materials. Judith Luna at Oxford University Press has, as always, been patient and helpful.

Introduction

THE young Oscar Wilde left Dublin for Oxford in 1874, and he never really lived in Ireland again. His father, an eminent surgeon and antiquarian, died while he was at Oxford, and his mother, whom he idolized, came to live in London in very reduced circumstances. She had been famous as Speranza, a poet of the Young Ireland movement of the 1840s, but now there seemed nothing in Ireland for her, her elder son Willie, or her younger son Oscar. Oscar prepared himself for change. His Irish accent, he declared, was one of the things he lost at Oxford. Later he saw the changes as pivotal: 'the two great turning-points of my life were when my father sent me to Oxford, and when society sent me to prison'.[1]

On the face of it, Wilde became an Englishman at Oxford. Oscar Browning wrote of his *Poems* in 1881 that: 'England is enriched with a new poet', and American reviewers particularly enjoyed his 'Ave Imperatrix', perhaps in part because of its republicanism: 'How an Englishman can read it without a glow of pride and sigh of sorrow is beyond comprehension.'[2] In the last hundred years he has repeatedly been described as an English writer, and there has been silent complicity in Ireland: most important works on Anglo-Irish literature have failed to treat him. Only recently has his basic Irish identity begun to be recognized, so that for example he is at last fully recognized in *The Field Day Anthology of Irish Writing* (1991). Declan Kiberd contributes a provocative essay to the second volume on this very question of Englishness and Irishness, and a generous selection of his work is included (but, interestingly, none of his poetry).[3]

But of course Oxford did not make Wilde an Englishman: nothing could do that. As Owen Dudley Edwards has put it, 'He was at once the metropolitan sophisticate and the loyal son of the Celtic periphery'.[4] He found the English too solemn and self-important to assimilate to them completely, and most of his best work testifies to that. But Oxford did go far to make the early

[1] Rupert Hart-Davis (ed.), *The Letters of Oscar Wilde* (1962), 469.
[2] Karl Beckson (ed.), *Oscar Wilde: The Critical Heritage* (1970), 4.
[3] Kiberd in *Field Day Anthology*, ii. 372–83; Wilde, 383–420.
[4] Introduction to *The Fireworks of Oscar Wilde* (1989), 30.

Wilde wear the mask of an English poet, although later as a prose-writer he retained the brilliant Irish–English wit that distinguished Congreve, Swift, and Sheridan. Irish contemporaries such as Yeats, Shaw, and Joyce never doubted his Irishness, or his consummate mockery of the English. But at Oxford and for a few years after the young poet discarded the passion and politics of his mother's rhetorical anti-Famine poetry, and instead served an appreciative apprenticeship to English poetry, to Shakespeare, Milton, Words-worth, Keats, Tennyson, Arnold, Swinburne, and the Pre-Raphaelites in particular. His early poetry was a eulogy of a particular English poetic tradition, nourished by the Classics. The subject-matter tended to be fairly traditional: beauty, love, faith, decorated stories in the Romantic tradition, rapt self-analysis and self-reproach.

Furthermore, although he was not centrally a political poet, the politics implicit or explicit in some of the *Poems* are startling, from a 'loyal son of the Celtic periphery', or indeed the son of his mother, 'Speranza'. In Wilde's ordering, they come in the first section, 'Eleutheria', concerned with political freedom. The much-praised 'Ave Imperatrix' is a tribute to a very English Empire, and catches the spirit of the time when Imperial soldiers were facing attacks from 'lesser breeds without the Law' on the far-flung edges of 'civilization'. Here the poet speaks of 'our English land', and invokes the name of Oliver Cromwell, a name which has provoked outrage in Ireland since Wexford and Drogheda:

> O Cromwell's England! must thou yield
> For every inch of ground a son?

'Quantum Mutata' also celebrates the time when 'England's lion leaping from its lair' went to the defence, under Cromwell, of the oppressed. And perhaps the most astonishing of all is the sonnet 'To Milton', which laments the loss of the high principles and spirit of Milton, and invokes Cromwell yet again in a final passage which seems to celebrate the suppression of Ireland:

> Dear God! is this the land
> Which bare a triple empire in her hand
> When Cromwell spake the word Democracy!

The only collection of poems Wilde was to publish, *Poems* (1881), brought very conflicting reactions, but not on grounds of nationality. Many accused it of obscenity, and by implication of perversity, citing 'Charmides' in particular, where a youth violates the sacred statue of the virgin goddess Athena. On the other hand, Wilde's long-term enemy, the satiric magazine *Punch*, declared, 'The poet is Wilde, | But his poetry's tame', and American Ambrose Bierce fulminated about 'the limpid and spiritless vacuity of this intellectual jellyfish'.[5] In the end, the strongest and most persistent charge was of plagiarism. When the volume was published, it was requested, as was usual, for the Library of the Oxford Union. But very unusually it was attacked in the full chamber, by Oliver Elton, later to be a professor of English:

It is not that these poems are thin—and they *are* thin: it is not that they are immoral—and they *are* immoral: it is not that they are this or that—and they *are* all this and all that: it is that they are for the most part not by their putative father at all, but by a number of better-known and more deservedly reputed authors. They are in fact by William Shakespeare, by Philip Sidney, by John Donne, by Lord Byron, by William Morris, by Algernon Swinburne, and by sixty more . . . The Union Library already contains better and fuller editions of all these poets: the volume which we are offered is theirs, not Mr Wilde's: and I move that it be not accepted.[6]

A poll of those present agreed with Elton by 188 to 128, and in a vote of the whole membership they agreed again, by a much narrower margin, 188 to 180: the volume was returned to Wilde. Unabashed by this, or some scathing reviews to the same effect, Wilde revised and reprinted the volume, his final 'Author's Edition' coming out as late as 1892, by which time he was the successful author of fiction, criticism, and *Lady Windermere's Fan*; clearly, in a position to suppress his youthful poetry, he saw no reason not to reissue the poems he had allowed into the volume.

This debate rattles on down the next hundred years or so. Arthur Ransome, Wilde's first serious book-length critic, argued that while the poetry was 'full of variations on other men's music . . . to describe a young poet's work as derivative is not the same thing as to condemn it'. He said that Wilde's openness about his sources renders accusations of plagiarism absurd. He went on to point out what a rich source of autobiography these poems are.[7] Arthur Symons talked of 'the exquisite echoes of the *Poems*',[8] while the indefatigable German scholar Bernhard Fehr in 1918 took

[5] Beckson, *Oscar Wilde*, 53.

[6] Quoted by Richard Ellmann, *Oscar Wilde* (1987), 140.

[7] Arthur Ransome, *Oscar Wilde* (1913), 38–45. [8] Beckson, *Oscar Wilde*, 94.

source-hunting to its logical extreme, when he reduced the long poem 'Humanitad' to a quasi-mathematical equation:

Humanitad = Matthew Arnold + Shelley's Sensitive Plant + Pater's Schlusswort + Swinburne's Dolores + Hesperia + Eve of Revolution + A Song of Italy + Siena + Halt before Rome + Super Flumina Babylonis + Perinde ac Cadaver + Morris's Anti-Scrape Society + Pater's Winckelmann + Swinburne's Before a Crucifix + The Hymn of Man + Hertha + Baudelaire's Héautontimoroumenos.[9]

More recent attention has been limited: Wilde's poetry has been overshadowed by his short stories, his novel, his plays, his critical dialogues, and of course his life, but critics continue to differ over the manifest indebtedness of the early *Poems*. In 1954 J. D. Thomas found the dominant characteristics of the early poems to be their sensuousness, and their concentration on colour: 'The result frequently is the effect of a Keats gone mad; even when Wilde succeeds, we feel very near to surfeit.'[10] In 1982 Averil Gardner was morally outraged by her discovery of Wilde's plagiarism of himself, and more by the echoes of other poets so long ago acknowledged:

But as one reads through *Poems* the number of verbal similarities leads to a hardening of critical attitude: one feels that Wilde was more than usually immature in his slavish regurgitation of diverse and unassimilated poetic tags; one is impatient with his lazy refusal to replace the shorthand of quotation by a carefully thought-out phrasing of his own; and one is shocked at the effrontery of a would-be literary impostor.

She goes on to rehearse 'the barefacedness of Wilde's pilfering' from Milton, and the 'most glaring example of daylight robbery from Arnold'.[11]

It was left to Jerome H. Buckley to restore the balance in a sensitive article called 'Echo and Artifice: The Poetry of Oscar Wilde' in 1990. He restates the general Ransome position: 'but echoing is not necessarily plagiarising', and goes on: 'The actor's voice in Wilde seems well pleased with its virtuosity in imitation. We sense behind it nothing of a plagiarist's evasions or anxieties of

    [9] Bernhard Fehr, 'Studien zu Oscar Wildes Gedichten', in *Palaestra*, 100 (1918), 32.
    [10] J. D. Thomas, 'Oscar Wilde's Prose and Poetry', *Rice Institute Pamphlet*, 42 (1954), 32–52, p. 47.
    [11] Averil Gardner, 'Literary Petty Larceny: Plagiarism in Oscar Wilde's Early Poetry', *English Studies in Canada*, 8 (1982), 52–4.

influence.' He looks seriously at the poems, and their development.
He stresses Wilde's long admiration for *In Memoriam*, and finds
169 examples of the 'In Memoriam stanza' in the 1908 edition of
Poems by Robert Ross.. But he points to the French titles of some
of these lyrics, particularly those with titles such as 'Impressions',
and shows that the dominant inspiration of these slightly later
poems is French rather than English.[12] We might say that the
stanza may still be that of Tennyson's *In Memoriam*, but the
inspiration owes more to Gautier's *Émaux et Camées*, which were
composed in even sparer quatrains. The contemporary reader is
better placed than previous generations to reassess the work of the
young poet.

This volume follows as closely as possible the chronological
order of composition, which was established by Professor Bobby
Fong. This highlights the elements of autobiography Ransome
pointed to, the young Wilde's conflicting attitudes to Greece and
Rome, pagan and Christian, and his fluctuating attraction to
Roman Catholicism. Necessarily, though, it sacrifices Wilde's
own ordering of the early volume, which has different principles
of shaping. Wilde had constructed the volume with great care
round a 'musical' arrangement of themes (see Appendix).

Wilde had published a number of short poems before the
volume of 1881, some of which he chose not to include in the
volume, but most of them appear. And having the scale of a volume
allowed him to produce for the occasion some long poems, such as
his Romantic predecessors had done, poems like 'Charmides', 'The
Burden of Itys', and 'The Garden of Eros'. He had the volume
published very attractively, at his own expense, and sent copies to
writers he admired, such as Robert Browning and Matthew
Arnold, and a politician such as Gladstone, whose help would be
potentially valuable. Thereafter he used it as a kind of visiting card,
for example with French writers whose acquaintance he made
during his stay in Paris in 1883.

After 1881 Wilde wrote much less poetry, but he did produce
some fine poems, such as 'The Harlot's House'. Buckley sees the
'Impressions' poems of 1881 as bringing 'the new Aesthetic note
into Victorian poetry', and 'The Harlot's House' moving into 'the
darker shadows of Decadence'. Wilde's best Decadent poem, by

[12] Jerome H. Buckley, 'Echo and Artifice: The Poetry of Oscar Wilde', *Victorian
Poetry*, 28 (1990), 19–31, at pp. 21, 24–6.

common consent, is *The Sphinx*, composed at intervals over many years. This poem has manifold French 'sources',[13] but I agree with Buckley that 'whatever its literary antecedents, *The Sphinx* emerges as Wilde's own exhibition of virtuosity and recondite reference'.[14] But the antecedents may not be simply literary: just as Gustave Moreau's paintings of Salome had an effect on Wilde, as well as Huysmans's descriptions of them in *A Rebours*, so *The Sphinx* may owe more than a little to Moreau's curious painting *Oedipus and the Sphinx*, exhibited in the Salon of 1864. Lothar Hönnighausen has described Moreau's aestheticist sphinx as 'characterised by the ambivalence of erotic fears and desires', and discussed the prevalence of the imagery of the sphinx in Pre-Raphaelite and *fin de siècle* poetry and painting.[15]

The one poem of Wilde's which most people have encountered is *The Ballad of Reading Gaol*. Ironically, it is the work of his that most thoroughly subverts most of his aesthetic tenets, that life imitates art, not the reverse, that 'in a very ugly and sensible age, the arts borrow not from life but from each other', that 'all art is useless', and that art and propaganda are incompatible. It is his only work directly inspired by life, by the execution for murder of a fellow inmate of HM Prison, Reading. And it had a 'phenomenal reception' on the Continent and in the United States, and has been multiply translated into every European language, and translated into several non-European languages, such as Hebrew, Japanese, and Arabic.[16]

Wilde himself was conscious as he wrote of a divided aim, of including propaganda against capital punishment, and against prisons. A particularly stringent critic, W. B. Yeats, pruned it from 109 stanzas to a mere 38 for *The Oxford Book of Modern Verse*, saying that the pure narrative was all that was strictly required, and even the famous declaration that 'each man kills the thing he loves' disappeared under his blue pencil. On the other hand, Albert Camus declared that prison had made Wilde—sadly briefly—a great artist, and only four years after his death his friend the

---

[13] See I. Murray, 'Some Problems of Editing Wilde's Poem *The Sphinx*', *Durham University Journal*, 82/1 (1990), 73–9.   [14] Buckley, 'Echo and Artifice', 27
[15] Lothar Hönnighausen, *The Symbolist Tradition in English Literature: A Study of Pre-Raphaelitism and* Fin de Siècle (1988), 232–9.
[16] Beckson, *Oscar Wilde*, 26–7.

poet Violet Fane wrote how a friend had compared Wilde with Dante:

He told me once that he would have placed certain passages in this poem, by reason of their terrible tragic intensity, upon a level with some of the descriptions in Dante's *Inferno*, were it not that '*The Ballad of Reading Gaol* was so much more *infinitely human*'![17]

The best recent essay on the *Ballad*—interestingly by a poet, is 'Speranza in Reading: On *The Ballad of Reading Gaol*' by Seamus Heaney.[18] Irish writers and critics have been making up for the long neglect, and Heaney sees the *Ballad* as anticipating in some senses the impact made on young poets by World War I. His exploration is subtle and perceptive, and not open to brief summary, but he does agree with Wilde that it suffers from 'a divided aim in style', and in the end he prefers Wilde's prose:

the axe which is still capable of shattering the surfaces of convention is neither the realistic ballad which Yeats fashioned nor the original romantic plea from which he extracted it; it is rather the hard-edged, unpathetic prose that Wilde created in dialogues like 'The Decay of Living' and dramas like *The Importance of Being Earnest*.[19]

But the rest of Wilde's poetry has been critically unfashionable for a long time; indeed, I suspect, unread, and this has spurred some critics, including the Irish, to what Heaney calls 'relish and extravagance'.[20] This has encouraged powerful, effective, and antithetical statements about Wilde's œuvre, which are not all as true as we might like them to be in the full context of his work. For example, Declan Kiberd, in both his 1984 Field Day pamphlet, *Anglo-Irish Attitudes*, and his essay in the *Field Day Anthology*, talks of Wilde 'in a lifelong performance of Englishness which constituted a parody of the very notion'.[21] But I have suggested that the 'Englishnesses' of the early poems, both the traditional, literary Englishness and the naïvely patriotic, Cromwell-praising Englishness, are not part of a masterful and premeditated plan. I suggest this was part of stumbling towards self-discovery—or self-creation—if only, as Kiberd and Heaney suggest, in a classic reaction

[17] Mary Montgomerie Currie, 'Concerning Some of the *Enfants Trouvés* of Literature', *Nineteenth Century* (July 1904), 133.

[18] Seamus Heaney, 'Speranza in Reading: On *The Ballad of Reading Gaol*', in *The Redress of Poetry* (1995), 83–102.   [19] Heaney, 'Speranza in Reading', 97.

[20] Ibid. 87.   [21] *Field Day Anthology*, ii. 374.

against one or both parents and all they stood for (Kiberd empha-
sizes Sir William; Heaney, Speranza).

Similarly, I earlier cited with approval Owen Dudley Edwards's
tempting antithesis about Wilde as at once a metropolitan sophis-
ticate and a loyal son of the Celtic periphery. But again it only fully
works or applies if we ignore most of the poetry, which Wilde
himself chose not to do. True, in his poetry he was sometimes both,
but he was sometimes neither: it was a hard balancing act, and not
the only one in which he was engaged. Wilde the poet is rarely a
metropolitan sophisticate: when he is, the metropolis has a flavour
of Paris, rather than London. This applies to a number of poems,
from 'Impression du Matin' and 'Fantaisies Décoratives', through
'The Harlot's House' to *The Sphinx*. The alternative, for Wilde the
poet generally and Wilde the early poet in particular, is not to write
poetry as a loyal son of the Celtic periphery, but to try on voices, to
search for a voice in a tradition which is foreign to him, to perform
Englishness and Romanticism as if in search for a place for his
individual talent, in a fashion insufficiently assured to be described
as parody, whatever mastery of parody he was to achieve in prose
thereafter.

Wilde's poetry generally strives for an individual voice that is
only distantly related to the authentic prose voice, so widely and
rightly admired. I see in the poetry a constant development
towards that voice. It is perhaps possible to go along with what
both he and Seamus Heaney say about a divided aim in style, and
still see the *Ballad* as not a failure but a triumph. True, it defies his
earlier artistic aims, but he never believed in consistency. Certainly
this poem, which Heaney calls 'haunting, problematical', is to be
celebrated, as a summative work which achieves perhaps the most
effective, and the most dangerous, balancing act of his career.
Heaney again:

The relatively objective ballad which Yeats excerpted from the original
does have a powerful and passionate quality of the kind that he himself
would have aimed for; but the ballad which Wilde wrote, while it is more
self-indulgent and confiding, lodges a plea and generates a sympathy
which are uniquely disturbing.[22]

[22] Heaney, 'Speranza in Reading', 102.

Chronology

1854 Oscar Wilde born in Dublin, second son of distinguished parents, both authors, Dr (later Sir) William Wilde, leading oculist and ear-surgeon, and Jane Francesca Elgee, poet and translator, who wrote for the Young Ireland movement of the 1840s, under the name Speranza.

1864–71 At Portora Royal School, Enniskillen.

1867 Death of Wilde's younger sister Isola, aged eight.

1871–4 At Trinity College, Dublin, reading Classics.

1873 Publication of the first edition of Pater's *Renaissance*, with its notorious and far-reaching 'Conclusion'.

1874 Berkeley Gold Medal for Greek at Trinity; matriculates, with a scholarship, at Magdalen College, Oxford.

1875 Summer: visits Italy with Dublin professor J. P. Mahaffy. November: first published poem, 'Chorus of Cloud-Maidens' in *Dublin University Magazine*. Many poems published hereafter, not all chosen for inclusion in *Poems* (1881).

1876 Death of Sir William Wilde. Wilde takes a First Class in Classical Moderations.

1877 Spring vacation: visits Genoa, Ravenna, and then Greece with Mahaffy, seeing Corfu, Olympia, Argos, Aegina, Athens, and Mycenae. Returns by Rome.

1878 Wins the Newdigate Prize for his poem *Ravenna*. Takes a First Class in *Litterae Humaniores*.

1879 Settles in London, as 'professor' of aesthetics: regularly lampooned in *Punch* from now on.

1881 *Poems* published: three small identical editions. Gilbert and Sullivan's light opera *Patience* produced, satirizing the aesthetes.

1882 Fourth and fifth editions of *Poems*, with significant revisions. Spends year lecturing in United States and Canada, on such subjects as 'The English Renaissance of Art' and 'The House Beautiful'.

1883 Three months in Paris; lectures in Britain; the early play *Vera* rather unsuccessfully produced in New York.

1884 Marries Constance Lloyd; settles in Chelsea. Begins regular book-reviewing, which continues until 1890. Publishes occasional poems until 1889.

1885 Son Cyril born. Passing of the Criminal Law Amendment Act 1885, which for the first time prohibited indecent relations between consenting males, the offence for which Wilde would serve his years in prison.

1886   Wilde meets Robert Ross. Son Vyvyan born.
1887–9   Edits *The Woman's World*.
1888   *The Happy Prince and Other Tales* published.
1889   'The Portrait of Mr W. H.' published in *Blackwood's*.
1890   The first version of *Dorian Gray* published in *Lippincott's Monthly Magazine*.
1891   Meets Lord Alfred Douglas. An early play *The Duchess of Padua* produced in New York as *Guido Ferranti*. Publishes the revised and expanded *Dorian Gray, Intentions, Lord Arthur Savile's Crime and Other Stories, A House of Pomegranates*. 'The Soul of Man under Socialism' published in the *Fortnightly Review*. Irish political leader Parnell, having been vindicated on charges of political murder, is publicly ruined because of his involvement in a divorce suit.
1892   *Lady Windermere's Fan* produced. *Salome* is refused a licence for production in London by Sarah Bernhardt.
1893   *Salome* (original French version) published in Paris. *A Woman of No Importance* is produced in London and *Lady Windermere's Fan* is published.
1894   *Salome* is published in English translation, with illustrations by Aubrey Beardsley. *The Sphinx* and *A Woman of No Importance* published.
1895   *An Ideal Husband* and *The Importance of Being Earnest* produced in London. Wilde charges Lord Alfred Douglas's father, the Marquess of Queensberry, with criminal libel. On Queensberry's acquittal, Wilde is arrested for 'acts of gross indecency with other male persons'. The first trial jury fails to agree a verdict: at the second trial Wilde is found guilty and given the maximum sentence, two years hard labour, and sent to Pentonville. He is moved to Wandsworth, and finally to Reading Prison. He is declared bankrupt.
1896   Death of Lady Wilde: Constance Wilde travels from Genoa to Reading Prison to break the news. *Salome* produced in Paris.
1897   Writes *De Profundis* (a long letter to Lord Alfred Douglas) in prison. On his release Wilde writes to the *Daily Chronicle* about the treatment of children in prison. He settles first at Berneval, near Dieppe; later he joins Lord Alfred Douglas in Italy, causing a new rift with his family.
1898   Moves to Paris. Publishes *The Ballad of Reading Gaol* anonymously, and writes another long letter about prison conditions to the *Daily Chronicle*. Death of Constance Wilde.
1899   *The Importance of Being Earnest* and *An Ideal Husband* published. Travels in Europe.
1900   Visits Rome, returns to Paris. During serious illness is baptized a Roman Catholic: dies 30 November.

Note on the Text

The editor is indebted to Professor Bobby Fong for permission to follow the chronological order of Wilde's poems as established in his unpublished critical edition of 1978. This gives a much clearer picture of Wilde's poetic development, and of his fluctuating religious and political ideas than Wilde's own careful grouping and structuring of the early volume, *Poems*, 1881. However, that grouping was retained by Wilde as late as 1892, when the last sheets were reissued as 'The Author's Edition'. The schema as elaborated by Wilde for 1882 is given in the Appendix.

The general principle of this edition is that it includes all the poems Wilde printed in books (*Ravenna*, *Poems* (1881, etc.), *The Sphinx*, and *The Ballad of Reading Gaol*), plus other poems he completed and published elsewhere, but not unfinished poems, or others implicitly rejected or deliberately uncollected. I have compared Wilde's revised edition of *Poems* (1882), Robert Ross's edition of 1908, and Fong's of 1978, and made use of Stuart Mason's *Bibliography of Oscar Wilde* (1914).

Professor Fong also generously invited me to use such of his explanatory notes as suited my purposes, and I have gratefully done so in some cases.

Chorus of Cloud-Maidens

(Ἀριστοφανοῦς Νεφέλαι, 275–290, 298–313)[1]

Στροφή[2]

Cloud-maidens that float on for ever,
   Dew-sprinkled, fleet bodies, and fair,
Let us rise from our Sire's loud river,
   Great Ocean, and soar through the air
To the peaks of the pine-covered mountains where the pines
      hang as tresses of hair.
Let us seek the watchtowers undaunted,
   Where the well-watered cornfields abound,
And through murmurs of rivers nymph-haunted
   The songs of the sea-waves resound;
And the sun in the sky never wearies of spreading his
      radiance around.   10
     Let us cast off the haze
     Of the mists from our band,
     Till with far-seeing gaze
     We may look on the land.

[1] Aristophanes, *The Clouds*
[2] Strophe

Ἀντιστροφή[1]

Cloud-maidens that bring the rain-shower,
   To the Pallas-loved land let us wing,
To the land of stout heroes and Power,
   Where Kekrops was hero and king,
Where honour and silence is given
   To the mysteries that none may declare,   20
Where are gifts to the high gods in heaven
   When the house of the gods is laid bare,
Where are lofty roofed temples, and statues well carven
      and fair;
   Where are feasts to the happy immortals

[1] Antistrophe

When the sacred procession draws near,
  Where garlands make bright the high portals
At all seasons and months in the year;
  And when spring days are here,
Then we tread to the wine-god a measure,
  In Bacchanal dance and in pleasure,   30
'Mid the contests of sweet singing choirs,
  And the crash of loud lyres.

Oxford, 1874

From Spring Days to Winter
(For Music)

In the glad spring when leaves were green,
  O merrily the throstle sings!
I sought, amid the tangled sheen,
Love whom mine eyes had never seen,
  O the glad dove has golden wings!

Between the blossoms red and white,
  O merrily the throstle sings!
My love first came into my sight,
O perfect vision of delight,
  O the glad dove has golden wings!   10

The yellow apples glowed like fire.
  O merrily the throstle sings!
O Love too great for lip or lyre,
Blown rose of love and of desire,
  O the glad dove has golden wings!

But now with snow the tree is grey
  Ah, sadly now the throstle sings!
My love is dead: ah! well-a-day,

See at her silent feet I lay
    A dove with broken wings!   20
Ah, Love! ah, Love! that thou wert slain—
Fond Dove, fond Dove return again.

Magdalen College, Oxford

Requiescat

Tread lightly, she is near
    Under the snow,
Speak gently, she can hear
    The daisies grow.

All her bright golden hair
    Tarnished with rust,
She that was young and fair
    Fallen to dust.

Lily-like, white as snow,
    She hardly knew   10
She was a woman, so
    Sweetly she grew.

Coffin-board, heavy stone,
    Lie on her breast,
I vex my heart alone,
    She is at rest.

Peace, Peace, she cannot hear
    Lyre or sonnet,
All my life's buried here,
    Heap earth upon it.   20

Avignon

San Miniato

See, I have climbed the mountain side
Up to this holy house of God,
Where once that Angel-Painter trod
Who saw the heavens opened wide,

And throned upon the crescent moon
The Virginal white Queen of Grace,—
Mary! could I but see thy face
Death could not come at all too soon.

O crowned by God with thorns and pain!
Mother of Christ! O mystic wife!　　　　10
My heart is weary of this life
And over-sad to sing again.

O crowned by God with love and flame!
O crowned by Christ the Holy One!
O listen ere the searching sun
Show to the world my sin and shame.

By the Arno

The oleander on the wall
Grows crimson in the dawning light,
Though the grey shadows of the night
Lie yet on Florence like a pall.

The dew is bright upon the hill,
And bright the blossoms overhead,
But ah! the grasshoppers have fled,
The little Attic song is still.

Only the leaves are gently stirred
By the soft breathing of the gale,　　　　10
And in the almond-scented vale
The lonely nightingale is heard.

The day will make thee silent soon,
O nightingale sing on for love!
While yet upon the shadowy grove
Splinter the arrows of the moon.

Before across the silent lawn
In sea-green vest the morning steals,
And to love's frightened eyes reveals
The long white fingers of the dawn   20

Fast climbing up the eastern sky
To grasp and slay the shuddering night,
All careless of my heart's delight,
Or if the nightingale should die.

Rome Unvisited

i

The corn has turned from grey to red,
    Since first my spirit wandered forth
    From the drear cities of the north,
And to Italia's mountains fled.

And here I set my face towards home,
    For all my pilgrimage is done,
    Although, methinks, yon blood-red sun
Marshals the way to Holy Rome.

O Blessed Lady, who dost hold
    Upon the seven hills thy reign!
    O Mother without blot or stain,   10
Crowned with bright crowns of triple gold!

O Roma, Roma, at thy feet
    I lay this barren gift of song!
    For, ah! the way is steep and long
That leads unto thy sacred street.

II

And yet what joy it were for me
  To turn my feet unto the south,
  And journeying towards the Tiber mouth
To kneel again at Fiesole!   20

And wandering through the tangled pines
  That break the gold of Arno's stream,
  To see the purple mist and gleam
Of morning on the Apennines.

By many a vineyard-hidden home,
  Orchard, and olive-garden grey,
  Till from the drear Campagna's way
The seven hills bear up the dome!

III

A pilgrim from the northern seas—
  What joy for me to seek alone   30
  The wondrous Temple, and the throne
Of Him who holds the awful keys!

When, bright with purple and with gold,
  Come priest and holy Cardinal,
  And borne above the heads of all
The gentle Shepherd of the Fold.

O joy to see before I die
  The only God-anointed King,
  And hear the silver trumpets ring
A triumph as He passes by!   40

Or at the brazen-pillared shrine
  Holds high the mystic sacrifice,
  And shows his God to human eyes
Beneath the veil of bread and wine.

IV

For lo, what changes time can bring!
  The cycles of revolving years
  May free my heart from all its fears,
And teach my lips a song to sing.

Before yon field of trembling gold
  Is garnered into dusty sheaves,   50
  Or ere the autumn's scarlet leaves
Flutter as birds adown the wold,

I may have run the glorious race,
  And caught the torch while yet aflame,
  And called upon the holy name
Of Him who now doth hide His face.

Arona

La Bella Donna Della Mia Mente

My limbs are wasted with a flame,
  My feet are sore with travelling,
For calling on my Lady's name
  My lips have now forgot to sing.

O Linnet in the wild-rose brake
  Strain for my Love thy melody,
O Lark sing louder for love's sake,
  My gentle Lady passeth by.

She is too fair for any man
  To see or hold his heart's delight,   10
Fairer than Queen or courtezan
  Or moon-lit water in the night.

Her hair is bound with myrtle leaves,
  (Green leaves upon her golden hair!)
Green grasses through the yellow sheaves
  Of autumn corn are not more fair.

Her little lips, more made to kiss
  Than to cry bitterly for pain,
Are tremulous as brook-water is,
  Or roses after evening rain.   20

Her neck is like white melilote
  Flushing for pleasure of the sun,
The throbbing of the linnet's throat
  Is not so sweet to look upon.

As a pomegranate, cut in twain,
  White-seeded, is her crimson mouth,
Her cheeks are as the fading stain
  Where the peach reddens to the south.

O twining hands! O delicate
  White body made for love and pain!   30
O House of love! O desolate
  Pale flower beaten by the rain!

Chanson

A ring of gold and a milk-white dove
  Are goodly gifts for thee,
And a hempen rope for your own love
  To hang upon a tree.

For you a House of Ivory
  (Roses are white in the rose-bower)!
A narrow bed for me to lie
  (White, O white, is the hemlock flower)!

Myrtle and jessamine for you
  (O the red rose is fair to see)!
For me the cypress and the rue   10
  (Fairest of all is rose-mary)!

For you three lovers of your hand
    (Green grass where a man lies dead)!
For me three paces on the sand
    (Plant lilies at my head)!

The Dole of the King's Daughter
(Breton)

Seven stars in the still water,
    And seven in the sky;
Seven sins on the King's daughter,
    Deep in her soul to lie.

Red roses are at her feet,
    (Roses are red in her red–gold hair)
And O where her bosom and girdle meet
    Red roses are hidden there.

Fair is the knight who lieth slain
    Amid the rush and reed,   10
See the lean fishes that are fain
    Upon dead men to feed.

Sweet is the page that lieth there,
    (Cloth of gold is goodly prey,)
See the black ravens in the air,
    Black, O black as the night are they.

What do they there so stark and dead?
    (There is blood upon her hand.)
Why are the lilies flecked with red?
    (There is blood on the river sand.)   20

There are two that ride from the south and east,
    And two from the north and west,
For the black raven a goodly feast,
    For the King's daughter rest.

There is one man who loves her true,
  (Red, O red, is the stain of gore!)
He hath duggen a grave by the darksome yew,
  (One grave will do for four.)

No moon in the still heaven,
  In the black water none,
The sins on her soul are seven,   30
  The sin upon his is one.

Αἴλινον, αἴλινον εἰπέ, τὸ δ' εὖ νικάτω[1]

O well for him who lives at ease
  With garnered gold in wide domain,
  Nor heeds the splashing of the rain,
The crashing down of forest trees.

O well for him who ne'er hath known
  The travail of the hungry years,
  A father grey with grief and tears,
A mother weeping all alone.

But well for him whose feet have trod
  The weary road of earthly strife   10
  Yet from the sorrows of his life
Builds ladders to be nearer God.

S. M. Magdalen College, Oxford

  [1] Cry woe, woe, and let the good prevail

The True Knowledge

... ἀναγκαίως δ' ἔχει
βίον θερίζειν ὥστε κάρπιμον στάχυν,
καὶ τὸν μὲν εἶναι τὸν δὲ μή.[1]

Thou knowest all: —I seek in vain
    What lands to till or sow with seed;
    The land is black with briar and weed,
Nor cares for falling tears or rain.

Thou knowest all: —I sit and wait
    With blinded eyes and hands that fail,
    Till the last lifting of the veil
That hangs before God's holy gate.

Thou knowest all: —I cannot see;
    I trust I shall not live in vain:
    I *know* that we shall meet again
In some divine eternity.

S. M. Magdalen College, Oxford

[1] And like the grassy leas | In the morning, Life is mown; and this man is, | And that is not.

Θρηνωιδία[2]
(Eur. *Hec.*, 444–483)

Song sung by captive women of Troy on the sea beach at Aulis, while the Achæans were there storm-bound through the wrath of dishonoured Achilles, and waiting for a fair wind to bring them home.

Στροφη[3]

O fair wind blowing from the sea!
    Who through the dark and mist dost guide
    The ships that on the billows ride,

[2] Lamentation
[3] Strophe

Unto what land, ah, misery!
Shall I be borne, across what stormy wave,
Or to whose house a purchased slave?

O sea-wind blowing fair and fast
   Is it unto the Dorian strand,
     Or to those far and fabled shores,
     Where great Apidanus outpours   10
   His streams upon the fertile land,
   Or shall I tread the Phthian sand,
Borne by the swift breath of the blast.

Αντιστροφη[1]

O blowing wind! you bring my sorrow near,
   For surely borne with splashing of the oar,
And hidden in some galley-prison drear
   I shall be led unto that distant shore
     Where the tall palm-tree first took root, and made,
     With clustering laurel leaves, a pleasant shade
For Leto when with travail great she bore   20
     A god and goddess in Love's bitter fight,
     Her body's anguish, and her soul's delight.

     It may be in Delos,
       Encircled of seas,
     I shall sing with some maids
       From the Kyklades,
     Of Artemis goddess
       And queen and maiden,
     Sing of the gold
       In her hair heavy laden.   30
     Sing of her hunting,
       Her arrows and bow,
     And in singing find solace
       From weeping and woe.

[1] Antistrophe

Στροφη β

Or it may be my bitter doom
To stand a handmaid at the loom,
In distant Athens of supreme renown;
And weave some wondrous tapestry,
Or work in bright embroidery
Upon the crocus-flower'd robe and saffron-colour'd
gown, 40
The flying horses wrought in gold,
The silver chariot onward roll'd
That bears Athena through the Town;
Or the warring giants that strove to climb
From earth to heaven to reign as kings,
And Zeus the conquering son of Time
Borne on the hurricane's eagle wings;
And the lightning flame and the bolts that fell
From the risen cloud at the god's behest,
And hurl'd the rebels to darkness of hell, 50
To a sleep without slumber or waking or rest.

Αντιστροφη β

Alas! our children's sorrow, and their pain
In slavery.
Alas! our warrior sires nobly slain
For liberty.
Alas! our country's glory, and the name
Of Troy's fair town;
By the lances and the fighting and the flame
Tall Troy is down.

I shall pass with my soul overladen, 60
To a land far away and unseen,
For Asia is slave and handmaiden,
Europe is Mistress and Queen.
Without love, or love's holiest treasure,

I shall pass unto Hades abhorr'd,
To the grave as my chamber of pleasure,
To death as my Lover and Lord.

Lotus Leaves

νεμεσσῶμαί γε μὲν οὐδέν
κλαίειν ὅς κε θάνῃσι βροτῶν καὶ πότμον ἐπίσπῃ,
τοῦτό νυ καὶ γέρας οἶον ὀϊζυροῖσι βροτοῖσι
κείρασθαί τε κόμην βαλέειν τ' ἀπὸ δάκρυ παρειῶν. [1]

I

There is no peace beneath the noon.—
    Ah! in those meadows is there peace
    Where, girdled with a silver fleece,
As a bright shepherd, strays the moon?

Queen of the gardens of the sky,
    Where stars like lilies, white and fair,
    Shine through the mists of frosty air,
O tarry, for the dawn is nigh!

O tarry, for the envious day
    Stretches long hands to catch thy feet.   10
    Alas! but thou art overfleet,
Alas! I know thou wilt not stay.

II

Eastward the dawn has broken red,
    The circling mists and shadows flee;
    Aurora rises from the sea,
And leaves the crocus-flowered bed.

---

[1] Count it indeed no blame to weep for any mortal who has died and met his fate.
Yea, this is the only due we pay to miserable mortals, to cut the hair and let a tear
fall from the cheeks.

Eastward the silver arrows fall,
  Splintering the veil of holy night;
  And a long wave of yellow light
Breaks silently on tower and hall,   20

And spreading wide across the wold,
  Wakes into flight some fluttering bird;
  And all the chestnut tops are stirred,
And all the branches streaked with gold.

III

To outer senses there is peace,
  A dream-like peace on either hand;
  Deep silence in the shadowy land,
Deep silence where the shadows cease,

Save for a cry that echoes shrill
  From some lone bird disconsolate;   30
  A curlew calling to its mate;
The answer from the distant hill.

And, herald of my love to Him
  Who, waiting for the dawn, doth lie,
  The orbéd maiden leaves the sky,
And the white fires grow more dim.

IV

Up sprang the sun to run his race,
  The breeze blew fair on meadow and lea;
  But in the west I seemed to see
The likeness of a human face.   40

A linnet on the hawthorn spray
  Sang of the glories of the spring,
  And made the flow'ring copses ring
With gladness for the new-born day.

A lark from out the grass I trod
   Flew wildly, and was lost to view
   In the great seamless veil of blue
That hangs before the face of God.

The willow whispered overhead
   That death is but a newer life,   50
   And that with idle words of strife
We bring dishonour on the dead.

I took a branch from off the tree,
   And hawthorn-blossoms drenched with dew,
   I bound them with a sprig of yew,
And made a garland fair to see.

I laid the flowers where He lies
   (Warm leaves and flowers on the stone);
   What joy I had to sit alone
Till evening broke on tired eyes: 60

Till all the shifting clouds had spun
   A robe of gold for God to wear,
   And into seas of purple air
Sank the bright galley of the sun.

V

Shall I be gladdened for the day,
   And let my inner heart be stirred
   By murmuring tree or song of bird,
And sorrow at the wild wind's play?

Not so: such idle dreams belong
   To souls of lesser depth than mine;   70
   I feel that I am half divine;
I know that I am great and strong.

> I know that every forest tree
>   By labour rises from the root;
>   I know that none shall gather fruit
> By sailing on the barren sea.

S. M. Magdalen College, Oxford

A Fragment from the Agamemnon of Aeschylos

(Lines 1140–1173)

[The scene is the courtyard of the Palace at Argos. Agamemnon has already entered the House of Doom, and Klytaemnestra has followed close on his heels: —Kasandra is left alone upon the stage. The conscious terror of death, and the burden of prophecy, lie heavy upon her; terrible signs and visions greet her approach. She sees blood upon the lintel, and the smell of blood scares her, as some bird, from the door. The ghosts of the murdered children come to mourn with her. Her second sight pierces the palace walls; she sees the fatal bath, the trammelling net, and the axe sharpened for her own ruin and her lord's.

But not even in the hour of her last anguish is Apollo merciful; her warnings are unheeded; her prophetic utterances made mock of.

The orchestra is filled with a chorus of old men, weak, foolish, irresolute. They do not believe the weird woman of mystery till the hour for help is past, and the cry of Agamemnon echoes from the house, 'Oh me! I am stricken with a stroke of death.']

Χοπος[1]

> Thy prophecies are but a lying tale,
>   For cruel gods have brought thee to this state,
> And of thyself, and thine own wretched fate,
>   Sing you this song, and these unhallow'd lays,
> Like the brown bird of grief insatiate
>   Crying for sorrow of its dreary days;
> Crying for Itys, Itys, in the vale—
>   The nightingale! the nightingale!

[1] Chorus

Κασανδρα[1]

Yet I would that to me they had given
    The fate of that singer so clear,   10
Fleet wings to fly up into heaven,
    Away from all mourning and fear;
        For ruin and slaughter await me—the cleaving with
    sword and with spear.

Χορος

Whence come these crowding fancies on thy brain,
    Sent by some god it may be, yet for nought?
Why dost thou sing with evil-tongued refrain,—
Moulding thy terrors to this hideous strain
    With shrill sad cries, as if by death distraught?
Why dost thou tread that path of prophecy,
    Where, upon either hand,   20
    Landmarks for ever stand,
With horrid legend for all men to see?

Κασανδρα

O bitter bridegroom, who did'st bear
    Ruin to those that loved thee true!
O holy stream Skamander, where
    With gentle nurturement I grew
    In the first days, when life and love were new.

[1] Kasandra

And now—and now—it seems that I must lie
In the dark land that never sees the sun;
Sing my sad songs of fruitless prophecy,   30
　By the black stream Kokutos, that doth run
Through long low hills of dreary Acheron.

Χορος

Ah, but thy word is clear!
Even a child among men,
Even a child, might see
What is lying hidden here.
Ah! I am smitten deep
To the heart with a deadly blow!
At the evil fate of the maid,
At the cry of her song of woe;   40
Sorrows for her to bear!
Wonders for me to hear!

Κασανδρα

O my poor land, laid waste with flame and fire!
　O ruin'd city, overthrown by fate!
Ah, what avail'd the offerings of my Sire
　To keep the foreign foemen from the gate!
Ah, what avail'd the herds of pasturing kine
To save my country from the wrath divine!

Ah, neither prayer or priest availèd aught,
Nor the strong captains that so stoutly fought,   50
　For the tall town lies desolate and low.
　And I, the singer of this song of woe,
Know by the fire burning in my brain,
That Death, the healer of all earthly pain,
　Is close at hand. I will not shirk the blow.

A Vision

Two crownèd Kings, and One that stood alone
  With no green weight of laurels round his head,
  But with sad eyes as one uncomforted,
And wearied with man's never-ceasing moan
For sins no bleating victim can atone,
  And sweet long lips with tears and kisses fed.
  Girt was he in a garment black and red,
And at his feet I marked a broken stone
  Which sent up lilies, dove-like, to his knees.
  Now at their sight, my heart being lit with flame   10
I cried to Beatricé, 'Who are these?'
And she made answer, knowing well each name,
  'Æschylos first, the second Sophokles,
  And last (wide stream of tears!) Euripides.'

Sonnet on Approaching Italy

I reached the Alps: the soul within me burned,
  Italia, my Italia, at thy name:
  And when from out the mountain's heart I came
And saw the land for which my life had yearned,
I laughed as one who some great prize had earned:
  And musing on the marvel of thy fame
  I watched the day, till marked with wounds of flame
The turquoise sky to burnished gold was turned.
The pine-trees waved as waves a woman's hair,
  And in the orchards every twining spray   10
  Was breaking into flakes of blossoming foam:
But when I knew that far away at Rome
  In evil bonds a second Peter lay,
  I wept to see the land so very fair.

Turin

Sonnet
Written in Holy Week at Genoa

I wandered through Scoglietto's far retreat,
   The oranges on each o'erhanging spray
   Burned as bright lamps of gold to shame the day;
Some startled bird with fluttering wings and fleet
Made snow of all the blossoms, at my feet
   Like silver moons the pale narcissi lay:
   And the curved waves that streaked the great green bay
Laughed i' the sun, and life seemed very sweet.
Outside the young boy-priest passed singing clear,
   'Jesus the Son of Mary has been slain,   10
   O come and fill his sepulchre with flowers.'
Ah, God! Ah, God! those dear Hellenic hours
   Had drowned all memory of Thy bitter pain,
   The Cross, the Crown, the Soldiers, and the Spear.

Impression de Voyage

The sea was sapphire coloured, and the sky
   Burned like a heated opal through the air;
   We hoisted sail; the wind was blowing fair
For the blue lands that to the Eastward lie.
From the steep prow I marked with quickening eye
   Zakynthos, every olive grove and creek,
   Ithaca's cliff, Lycaon's snowy peak,
And all the flower-strewn hills of Arcady.
The flapping of the sail against the mast,
   The ripple of the water on the side,   10
   The ripple of girls' laughter at the stern,
The only sounds: —when 'gan the West to burn,
   And a red sun upon the seas to ride,
   I stood upon the soil of Greece at last!

Katakolo

The Theatre at Argos

Nettles and poppy mar each rock-hewn seat:
  No poet crowned with olive deathlessly
  Chants his glad song, nor clamorous Tragedy
Startles the air; green corn is waving sweet
Where once the Chorus danced to measures fleet;
  Far to the East a purple stretch of sea,
  The cliffs of gold that prisoned Danae;
And desecrated Argos at my feet.

No season now to mourn the days of old,
  A nation's shipwreck on the rocks of Time,   10
    Or the dread storms of all-devouring Fate,
    For now the peoples clamour at our gate,
  The world is full of plague and sin and crime,
And God Himself is half-dethroned for Gold!

Argos, 1877

Urbs Sacra Æterna

Rome! what a scroll of History thine has been;
  In the first days thy sword republican
  Ruled the whole world for many an age's span:
Then of the peoples wert thou royal Queen,
Till in thy streets the bearded Goth was seen;
  And now upon thy walls the breezes fan
  (Ah, city crowned by God, discrowned by man!)
The hated flag of red and white and green.
When was thy glory! when in search for power
  Thine eagles flew to greet the double sun,   10
    And the wild nations shuddered at thy rod?
Nay, but thy glory tarried for this hour,
  When pilgrims kneel before the Holy One,
  The prisoned shepherd of the Church of God.

Monte Mario

The Grave of Keats

Rid of the world's injustice, and his pain,
    He rests at last beneath God's veil of blue:
    Taken from life when life and love were new
The youngest of the Martyrs here is lain,
Fair as Sebastian, and as early slain.
    No cypress shades his grave, no funeral yew,
    But gentle violets weeping with the dew
Weave on his bones an ever-blossoming chain.
O proudest heart that broke for misery!
    O sweetest lips since those of Mitylene!
    O poet-painter of our English Land!
Thy name was writ in water—it shall stand:
    And tears like mine shall keep thy memory green,
    As Isabella did her Basil-tree.

Rome

Sonnet
on the Massacre of the Christians in Bulgaria

Christ, dost thou live indeed? or are thy bones
Still straitened in their rock-hewn sepulchre?
And was thy Rising only dreamed by Her
Whose love of thee for all her sin atones?
For here the air is horrid with men's groans,
The priests who call upon thy name are slain,
Dost thou not hear the bitter wail of pain
From those whose children lie upon the stones?
Come down, O Son of God! incestuous gloom
Curtains the land, and through the starless night
Over thy Cross a Crescent moon I see!
If thou in very truth didst burst the tomb
Come down, O Son of Man! and show thy might,
Lest Mahomet be crowned instead of Thee!

Easter Day

The silver trumpets rang across the Dome:
  The people knelt upon the ground with awe:
  And borne upon the necks of men I saw,
Like some great God, the Holy Lord of Rome.
Priest-like, he wore a robe more white than foam,
  And, king-like, swathed himself in royal red,
  Three crowns of gold rose high upon his head:
In splendour and in light the Pope passed home.
My heart stole back across wide wastes of years
  To One who wandered by a lonely sea,   10
  And sought in vain for any place of rest:
'Foxes have holes, and every bird its nest,
  I, only I, must wander wearily,
  And bruise my feet, and drink wine salt with tears.'

Sonnet
on Hearing the Dies Iræ Sung in the
Sistine Chapel

Nay, Lord, not thus! white lilies in the spring,
  Sad olive-groves, or silver-breasted dove,
  Teach me more clearly of Thy life and love
Than terrors of red flame and thundering.
The hillside vines dear memories of Thee bring:
  A bird at evening flying to its nest
  Tells me of One who had no place of rest:
I think it is of Thee the sparrows sing.
Come rather on some autumn afternoon,
  When red and brown are burnished on the leaves, 10
  And the fields echo to the gleaner's song,
Come when the splendid fulness of the moon
  Looks down upon the rows of golden sheaves,
  And reap Thy harvest: we have waited long.

Italia

Italia! thou art fallen, though with sheen
   Of battle-spears thy clamorous armies stride
   From the north Alps to the Sicilian tide!
Ay! fallen, though the nations hail thee Queen
Because rich gold in every town is seen,
   And on thy sapphire lake in tossing pride
   Of wind-filled vans thy myriad galleys ride
Beneath one flag of red and white and green.
O Fair and Strong! O Strong and Fair in vain!
   Look southward where Rome's desecrated town   10
   Lies mourning for her God-anointed King!
Look heaven-ward! shall God allow this thing?
   Nay! but some flame-girt Raphael shall come down,
   And smite the Spoiler with the sword of pain.

Venice

Vita Nuova

I stood by the unvintageable sea
   Till the wet waves drenched face and hair with spray;
   The long red fires of the dying day
Burned in the west; the wind piped drearily;
And to the land the clamorous gulls did flee:
   'Alas!' I cried, 'my life is full of pain,
   And who can garner fruit or golden grain
From these waste fields which travail ceaselessly!'
   My nets gaped wide with many a break and flaw,
   Nathless I threw them as my final cast   10
   Into the sea, and waited for the end.
When lo! a sudden glory! and I saw
   From the black waters of my tortured past
   The argent splendour of white limbs ascend!

E Tenebris

Come down, O Christ, and help me! reach thy hand,
  For I am drowning in a stormier sea
  Than Simon on thy lake of Galilee:
The wine of life is spilt upon the sand,
My heart is as some famine-murdered land
  Whence all good things have perished utterly,
  And well I know my soul in Hell must lie
If I this night before God's throne should stand.
'He sleeps perchance, or rideth to the chase,
  Like Baal, when his prophets howled that name   10
  From morn to noon on Carmel's smitten height.'
Nay, peace, I shall behold before the night,
  The feet of brass, the robe more white than flame,
  The wounded hands, the weary human face.

Quantum Mutata

There was a time in Europe long ago
  When no man died for freedom anywhere,
  But England's lion leaping from its lair
Laid hands on the oppressor! it was so
While England could a great Republic show.
  Witness the men of Piedmont, chiefest care
  Of Cromwell, when with impotent despair
The Pontiff in his painted portico
Trembled before our stern ambassadors.
  How comes it then that from such high estate   10
  We have thus fallen, save that Luxury
With barren merchandise piles up the gate
Where noble thoughts and deeds should enter by:
  Else might we still be Milton's heritors.

To Milton

Milton! I think thy spirit hath passed away
    From these white cliffs, and high-embattled towers;
    This gorgeous fiery-coloured world of ours
Seems fallen into ashes dull and grey,
And the age changed unto a mimic play
    Wherein we waste our else too-crowded hours:
    For all our pomp and pageantry and powers
We are but fit to delve the common clay,
Seeing this little isle on which we stand,
    This England, this sea-lion of the sea,   10
    By ignorant demagogues is held in fee,
Who love her not: Dear God! is this the land
    Which bare a triple empire in her hand
    When Cromwell spake the word Democracy!

Ave Maria Plena Gratia

Was this His coming! I had hoped to see
    A scene of wondrous glory, as was told
    Of some great God who in a rain of gold
Broke open bars and fell on Danae:
Or a dread vision as when Semele
    Sickening for love and unappeased desire
    Prayed to see God's clear body, and the fire
Caught her brown limbs and slew her utterly:
With such glad dreams I sought this holy place,
    And now with wondering eyes and heart I stand   10
    Before this supreme mystery of Love:
Some kneeling girl with passionless pale face,
    An angel with a lily in his hand,
    And over both the white wings of a Dove.

Florence

Wasted Days

(From A Picture Painted by Miss V. T.)

A fair slim boy not made for this world's pain,
  With hair of gold thick clustering round his ears,
  And longing eyes half veil'd by foolish tears
Like bluest water seen through mists of rain;
Pale cheeks whereon no kiss hath left its stain,
  Red under-lip drawn in for fear of Love,
  And white throat whiter than the breast of dove—
Alas! alas! if all should be in vain.

Corn-fields behind, and reapers all a-row
  In weariest labour toiling wearily,
  To no sweet sound of laughter, or of lute;
And careless of the crimson sunset-glow
  The boy still dreams: nor knows that night is nigh:
  And in the night-time no man gathers fruit.

Oxford, Oct. 30th

The Grave of Shelley

Like burnt-out torches by a sick man's bed
  Gaunt cypress-trees stand round the sun-bleached stone;
  Here doth the little night-owl make her throne,
And the slight lizard show his jewelled head.
And, where the chaliced poppies flame to red,
  In the still chamber of yon pyramid
  Surely some Old-World Sphinx lurks darkly hid,
Grim warder of this pleasaunce of the dead.

Ah! sweet indeed to rest within the womb
  Of Earth, great mother of eternal sleep,
But sweeter far for thee a restless tomb
  In the blue cavern of an echoing deep,
Or where the tall ships founder in the gloom
  Against the rocks of some wave-shattered steep.

Rome

Santa Decca

The Gods are dead: no longer do we bring
    To grey-eyed Pallas crowns of olive-leaves!
    Demeter's child no more hath tithe of sheaves,
And in the noon the careless shepherds sing,
For Pan is dead, and all the wantoning
    By secret glade and devious haunt is o'er:
    Young Hylas seeks the water-springs no more;
Great Pan is dead, and Mary's Son is King.

And yet—perchance in this sea-trancèd isle,
    Chewing the bitter fruit of memory,   10
    Some God lies hidden in the asphodel.
Ah love! if such there be then it were well
    For us to fly his anger: nay, but see
    The leaves are stirring: let us watch a-while.

Corfu

Theoretikos

This mighty empire hath but feet of clay:
    Of all its ancient chivalry and might
    Our little island is forsaken quite:
Some enemy hath stolen its crown of bay,
And from its hills that voice hath passed away
    Which spake of Freedom: O come out of it,
    Come out of it, my Soul, thou art not fit
For this vile traffic-house, where day by day
    Wisdom and reverence are sold at mart,
    And the rude people rage with ignorant cries   10
Against an heritage of centuries.
    It mars my calm: wherefore in dreams of Art
    And loftiest culture I would stand apart,
Neither for God, nor for his enemies.

Amor Intellectualis

Oft have we trod the vales of Castaly
  And heard sweet notes of sylvan music blown
  From antique reeds to common folk unknown:
And often launched our bark upon that sea
Which the nine Muses hold in empery,
  And ploughed free furrows through the wave and foam,
  Nor spread reluctant sail for more safe home
Till we had freighted well our argosy.
Of which despoilèd treasures these remain,
  Sordello's passion, and the honied line   10
Of young Endymion, lordly Tamburlaine
  Driving his pampered jades, and, more than these,
The seven-fold vision of the Florentine,
  And grave-browed Milton's solemn harmonies.

At Verona

How steep the stairs within Kings' houses are
  For exile-wearied feet as mine to tread,
  And O how salt and bitter is the bread
Which falls from this Hound's table,—better far
That I had died in the red ways of war,
  Or that the gate of Florence bare my head,
  Than to live thus, by all things comraded
Which seek the essence of my soul to mar.

'Curse God and die: what better hope than this?
  He hath forgotten thee in all the bliss   10
  Of his gold city, and eternal day'—
Nay peace: behind my prison's blinded bars
  I do possess what none can take away,
  My love, and all the glory of the stars.

Ravenna

A year ago I breathed the Italian air,—
And yet, methinks this northern Spring is fair,—
These fields made golden with the flower of March,
The throstle singing on the feathered larch,
The cawing rooks, the wood-doves fluttering by,
The little clouds that race across the sky;
And fair the violet's gentle drooping head,
The primrose, pale for love uncomforted,
The rose that burgeons on the climbing briar,
The crocus-bed, (that seems a moon of fire   10
Round-girdled with a purple marriage-ring);
And all the flowers of our English Spring,
Fond snow-drops, and the bright-starred daffodil.
Up starts the lark beside the murmuring mill,
And breaks the gossamer-threads of early dew;
And down the river, like a flame of blue,
Keen as an arrow flies the water-king,
While the brown linnets in the greenwood sing.
A year ago!—it seems a little time
Since last I saw that lordly southern clime,   20
Where flower and fruit to purple radiance blow,
And like the bright lamps the fabled apples glow.
Full Spring it was—and by rich flowering vines,
Dark olive-groves and noble forest-pines,
I rode at will; the moist glad air was sweet,
The white road rang beneath my horse's feet,
And musing on Ravenna's ancient name,
I watched the day till, marked with wounds of flame,
The turquoise sky to burnished gold was turned.

O how my heart with boyish passion burned,   30
When far away across the sedge and mere
I saw that Holy City rising clear,
Crowned with her crown of towers!—On and on
I galloped, racing with the setting sun,
And ere the crimson after-glow was passed,
I stood within Ravenna's walls at last!

II

How strangely still! no sound of life or joy
Startles the air; no laughing shepherd-boy
Pipes on his reed, nor ever through the day
Comes the glad sound of children at their play: 40
O sad, and sweet, and silent! surely here
A man might dwell apart from troublous fear,
Watching the tide of seasons as they flow
From amorous Spring to Winter's rain and snow,
And have no thought of sorrow;—here, indeed,
Are Lethe's waters, and that fatal weed
Which makes a man forget his fatherland.

Ay! amid lotus-meadows dost thou stand,
Like Proserpine, with poppy-laden head,
Guarding the holy ashes of the dead.   50
For though thy brood of warrior sons hath ceased,
Thy noble dead are with thee!—they at least
Are faithful to thine honour:—guard them well,
O childless city! for a mighty spell,
To wake men's hearts to dreams of things sublime,
Are the lone tombs where rest the Great of Time.

III

Yon lonely pillar, rising on the plain,
Marks where the bravest knight of France was slain,—
The Prince of chivalry, the Lord of war,
Gaston de Foix: for some untimely star   60
Led him against thy city, and he fell,
As falls some forest-lion fighting well.
Taken from life while life and love were new,
He lies beneath God's seamless veil of blue;
Tall lance-like reeds wave sadly o'er his head,
And oleanders bloom to deeper red,
Where his bright youth flowed crimson on the ground.

Look farther north unto that broken mound,—
There, prisoned now within a lordly tomb
Raised by a daughter's hand, in lonely gloom,   70
Huge-limbed Theodoric, the Gothic king,
Sleeps after all his weary conquering.
Time hath not spared his ruin,—wind and rain
Have broken down his stronghold; and again
We see that Death is mighty lord of all,
And king and clown to ashen dust must fall.

Mighty indeed *their* glory! yet to me
Barbaric king, or knight of chivalry,
Or the great queen herself, were poor and vain,
Beside the grave where Dante rests from pain.   80
His gilded shrine lies open to the air;
And cunning sculptor's hands have carven there
The calm white brow, as calm as earliest morn,
The eyes that flashed with passionate love and scorn,
The lips that sang of Heaven and of Hell,
The almond-face which Giotto drew so well,
The weary face of Dante;—to this day,
Here in his place of resting, far away
From Arno's yellow waters, rushing down
Through the wide bridges of that fairy town,   90
Where the tall tower of Giotto seems to rise
A marble lily under sapphire skies!
Alas! my Dante! thou hast known the pain
Of meaner lives,—the exile's galling chain,
How steep the stairs within kings' houses are,
And all the petty miseries which mar
Man's nobler nature with the sense of wrong.
Yet this dull world is grateful for thy song;
Our nations do thee homage,—even she,
That cruel queen of vine-clad Tuscany,   100
Who bound with crown of thorns thy living brow,
Hath decked thine empty tomb with laurels now,
And begs in vain the ashes of her son.

O mightiest exile! all thy grief is done:
Thy soul walks now beside thy Beatrice;
Ravenna guards thine ashes: sleep in peace.

IV

How lone this palace is; how grey the walls!
No minstrel now wakes echoes in these halls.
The broken chain lies rusting on the door,
And noisome weeds have split the marble floor: 110
Here lurks the snake, and here the lizards run
By the stone lions blinking in the sun.
Byron dwelt here in love and revelry
For two long years—a second Anthony,
Who of the world another Actium made!—
Yet suffered not his royal soul to fade,
Or lyre to break, or lance to grow less keen,
'Neath any wiles of an Egyptian queen.
For from the East there came a mighty cry,
And Greece stood up to fight for Liberty,   120
And called him from Ravenna: never knight
Rode forth more nobly to wild scenes of fight!
None fell more bravely on ensanguined field,
Borne like a Spartan back upon his shield!
O Hellas! Hellas! in thine hour of pride,
Thy day of might, remember him who died
To wrest from off thy limbs the trammelling chain:
O Salamis! O lone Platæan plain!
O tossing waves of wild Eubœan sea!
O wind-swept heights of lone Thermopylæ!   130
He loved you well—ay, not alone in word,
Who freely gave to thee his lyre and sword,
Like Æschylos at well-fought Marathon:

And England, too, shall glory in her son,
Her warrior-poet, first in song and fight.
No longer now shall Slander's venomed spite
Crawl like a snake across his perfect name,
Or mar the lordly scutcheon of his fame.

For as the olive-garland of the race,
Which lights with joy each eager runner's face,   140
As the red cross which saveth men in war,

As a flame-bearded beacon seen from far
By mariners upon a storm-tossed sea,—
Such was his love for Greece and Liberty!

Byron, thy crowns are ever fresh and green:
Red leaves of rose from Sapphic Mitylene
Shall bind thy brows; the myrtle blooms for thee,
In hidden glades by lonely Castaly;
The laurels wait thy coming: all are thine,
And round thy head one perfect wreath will twine.   150

V

The pine-tops rocked before the evening breeze
With the hoarse murmur of the wintry seas,
And the tall stems were streaked with amber bright;—
I wandered through the wood in wild delight,
Some startled bird, with fluttering wings and fleet,
Made snow of all the blossoms: at my feet,
Like silver crowns, the pale narcissi lay,
And small birds sang on every twining spray.
O waving trees, O forest liberty!
Within your haunts at least a man is free,   160
And half forgets the weary world of strife:
The blood flows hotter, and a sense of life
Wakes i' the quickening veins, while once again
The woods are filled with gods we fancied slain.
Long time I watched, and surely hoped to see
Some goat-foot Pan make merry minstrelsy
Amid the reeds! some startled Dryad-maid
In girlish flight! or lurking in the glade,
The soft brown limbs, the wanton treacherous face
Of woodland god! Queen Dian in the chase,   170
White-limbed and terrible, with look of pride,
And leash of boar-hounds leaping at her side!
Or Hylas mirrored in the perfect stream.

O idle heart! O fond Hellenic dream!
Ere long, with melancholy rise and swell,
The evening chimes, the convent's vesper-bell,
Struck on mine ears amid the amorous flowers.
Alas! alas! these sweet and honied hours
Had 'whelmed my heart like some encroaching sea,
And drowned all thoughts of black Gethsemane.   180

VI

O lone Ravenna! many a tale is told
Of thy great glories in the days of old:
Two thousand years have passed since thou didst see
Cæsar ride forth to royal victory,
Mighty thy name when Rome's lean eagles flew
From Britain's isles to far Euphrates blue;
And of the peoples thou wast noble queen,
Till in thy streets the Goth and Hun were seen.
Discrowned by man, deserted by the sea,
Thou sleepest, rocked in lonely misery!   190
No longer now upon thy swelling tide,
Pine-forest like, thy myriad galleys ride!
For where the brass-beaked ships were wont to float,
The weary shepherd pipes his mournful note;
And the white sheep are free to come and go
Where Adria's purple waters used to flow.

O fair! O sad! O Queen uncomforted!
In ruined loveliness thou liest dead,
Alone of all thy sisters; for at last
Italia's royal warrior hath passed   200
Rome's lordliest entrance, and hath worn his crown
In the high temples of the Eternal Town!
The Palatine hath welcomed back her king,
And with his name the seven mountains ring!

And Naples hath outlived her dream of pain,
And mocks her tyrant! Venice lives again,
New risen from the waters! and the cry

Of Light and Truth, of Love and Liberty,
Is heard in lordly Genoa, and where
The marble spires of Milan wound the air,   210
Rings from the Alps to the Sicilian shore,
And Dante's dream is now a dream no more.

But thou, Ravenna, better loved than all,
Thy ruined palaces are but a pall
That hides thy fallen greatness! and thy name
Burns like a grey and flickering candle-flame,
Beneath the noon-day splendour of the sun
Of new Italia! for the night is done,
The night of dark oppression, and the day
Hath dawned in passionate splendour: far away   220
The Austrian hounds are hunted from the land,
Beyond those ice-crowned citadels which stand
Girdling the plain of royal Lombardy,
From the far West unto the Eastern sea.

I know, indeed, that sons of thine have died
In Lissa's waters, by the mountain-side
Of Aspromonte, on Novara's plain,—
Nor have thy children died for thee in vain:
And yet, methinks, thou hast not drunk this wine
From grapes new-crushed of Liberty divine,   230
Thou hast not followed that immortal Star
Which leads the people forth to deeds of war.
Weary of life, thou liest in silent sleep,
As one who marks the lengthening shadows creep,
Careless of all the hurrying hours that run,
Mourning some day of glory, for the sun
Of Freedom hath not shewn to thee his face,
And thou hast caught no flambeau in the race.

Yet wake not from thy slumbers,—rest thee well,
Amidst thy fields of amber asphodel,   240
Thy lily-sprinkled meadows,—rest thee there,
To mock all human greatness: who would dare
To vent the paltry sorrows of his life
Before thy ruins, or to praise the strife
Of kings' ambition, and the barren pride

Of warring nations! wert not thou the Bride
Of the wild Lord of Adria's stormy sea!
The Queen of double Empires! and to thee
Were not the nations given as thy prey!
And now—thy gates lie open night and day,   250
The grass grows green on every tower and hall,
The ghastly fig hath cleft thy bastioned wall;
And where thy mailèd warriors stood at rest
The midnight owl hath made her secret nest.
O fallen! fallen! from thy high estate,
O city trammelled in the toils of Fate,
Doth nought remain of all thy glorious days,
But a dull shield, a crown of withered bays!

Yet who beneath this night of wars and fears,
From tranquil tower can watch the coming years;   260
Who can foretell what joys the day shall bring,
Or why before the dawn the linnets sing?
Thou, even thou, mayst wake, as wakes the rose
To crimson splendour from its grave of snows;
As the rich corn-fields rise to red and gold
From these brown lands, now stiff with Winter's cold;
As from the storm-rack comes a perfect star!

O much-loved city! I have wandered far
From the wave-circled islands of my home;
Have seen the gloomy mystery of the Dome   270
Rise slowly from the drear Campagna's way,
Clothed in the royal purple of the day:
I from the city of the violet crown
Have watched the sun by Corinth's hill go down,
And marked the 'myriad laughter' of the sea
From starlit hills of flower-starred Arkady;
Yet back to thee returns my perfect love,
As to its forest-nest the evening dove.

O poet's city! one who scarce has seen
Some twenty summers cast their doublets green,   280
For Autumn's livery, would seek in vain
To wake his lyre to sing a louder strain,
Or tell thy days of glory;—poor indeed

Is the low murmur of the shepherd's reed,
Where the loud clarion's blast should shake the sky,
And flame across the heavens! and to try
Such lofty themes were folly: yet I know
That never felt my heart a nobler glow
Than when I woke the silence of thy street
With clamorous trampling of my horse's feet,   290
And saw the city which now I try to sing,
After long days of weary travelling.

                          VII

    Adieu, Ravenna! but a year ago,
I stood and watched the crimson sunset glow
From the lone chapel on thy marshy plain:
The sky was as a shield that caught the stain
Of blood and battle from the dying sun,
And in the west the circling clouds had spun
A royal robe, which some great God might wear,
While into ocean-seas of purple air   300
Sank the gold galley of the Lord of Light.

    Yet here the gentle stillness of the night
Brings back the swelling tide of memory,
And wakes again my passionate love for thee:
Now is the Spring of Love, yet soon will come
On meadow and tree the Summer's lordly bloom;
And soon the grass with brighter flowers will blow,
And send up lilies for some boy to mow.
Then before long the Summer's conqueror,
Rich Autumn-time, the season's usurer,   310
Will lend his hoarded gold to all the trees,
And see it scattered by the spendthrift breeze;
And after that the Winter cold and drear.
So runs the perfect cycle of the year.
And so from youth to manhood do we go,
And fall to weary days and locks of snow.
Love only knows no winter; never dies:

Nor cares for frowning storms or leaden skies.
And mine for thee shall never pass away,
Though my weak lips may falter in my lay.   320

Adieu! Adieu! yon silent evening star,
The night's ambassador, doth gleam afar,
And bid the shepherd bring his flocks to fold.
Perchance before our inland seas of gold
Are garnered by the reapers into sheaves,
Perchance before I see the Autumn leaves,
I may behold thy city; and lay down
Low at thy feet the poet's laurel crown.

Adieu! Adieu! yon silver lamp, the moon,
Which turns our midnight into perfect noon,   330
Doth surely light thy towers, guarding well
Where Dante sleeps, where Byron loved to dwell.

Magdalen Walks

The little white clouds are racing over the sky,
    And the fields are strewn with the gold of the flower of March,
    The daffodil breaks under foot, and the tasselled larch
Sways and swings as the thrush goes hurrying by.

A delicate odour is borne on the wings of the morning breeze,
    The odour of deep wet grass, and of brown new-furrowed earth,
    The birds are singing for joy of the Spring's glad birth,
Hopping from branch to branch on the rocking trees.

And all the woods are alive with the murmur and sound of Spring,
    And the rosebud breaks into pink on the climbing briar,   10
    And the crocus-bed is a quivering moon of fire
Girdled round with the belt of an amethyst ring.

And the plane to the pine-tree is whispering some tale of love
    Till it rustles with laughter and tosses its mantle of green,
    And the gloom of the wych-elm's hollow is lit with the iris sheen
Of the burnished rainbow throat and the silver breast of a dove.

See! the lark starts up from his bed in the meadow there,
   Breaking the gossamer threads and the nets of dew,
   And flashing a-down the river, a flame of blue!
The kingfisher flies like an arrow, and wounds the air.   20

The Burden of Itys

This English Thames is holier far than Rome,
   Those harebells like a sudden flush of sea
Breaking across the woodland, with the foam
   Of meadow-sweet and white anemone
To fleck their blue waves,—God is likelier there,
Than hidden in that crystal-hearted star the pale monks bear!

Those violet-gleaming butterflies that take
   Yon creamy lily for their pavilion
Are monsignores, and where the rushes shake
   A lazy pike lies basking in the sun   10
His eyes half shut,—He is some mitred old
Bishop *in partibus*! look at those gaudy scales all green and gold.

The wind the restless prisoner of the trees
   Does well for Palæstrina, one would say
The mighty master's hands were on the keys
   Of the Maria organ, which they play
When early on some sapphire Easter morn
In a high litter red as blood or sin the Pope is borne

From his dark House out to the Balcony
   Above the bronze gates and the crowded square,   20
Whose very fountains seem for ecstasy
   To toss their silver lances in the air,
And stretching out weak hands to East and West
In vain sends peace to peaceless lands, to restless nations rest.

Is not yon lingering orange afterglow
   That stays to vex the moon more fair than all
Rome's lordliest pageants! strange, a year ago

I knelt before some crimson Cardinal
Who bare the Host across the Esquiline,
And now—those common poppies in the wheat seem twice as fine.

30

The blue-green beanfields yonder, tremulous
    With the last shower, sweeter perfume bring
Through this cool evening than the odorous
    Flame-jewelled censers the young deacons swing,
When the grey priest unlocks the curtained shrine,
And makes God's body from the common fruit of corn and vine.

Poor Fra Giovanni bawling at the mass
    Were out of tune now, for a small brown bird
Sings overhead, and through the long cool grass
    I see that throbbing throat which once I heard   40
On starlit hills of flower-starred Arcady,
Once where the white and crescent sand of Salamis meets sea.

Sweet is the swallow twittering on the eaves
    At daybreak, when the mower whets his scythe,
And stock-doves murmur, and the milkmaid leaves
    Her little lonely bed, and carols blithe
To see the heavy-lowing cattle wait
Stretching their huge and dripping mouths across the farmyard
    gate.

And sweet the hops upon the Kentish leas,
    And sweet the wind that lifts the new-mown hay,   50
And sweet the fretful swarms of grumbling bees
    That round and round the linden blossoms play;
And sweet the heifer breathing in the stall,
And the green bursting figs that hang upon the red-brick wall.

And sweet to hear the cuckoo mock the spring
    While the last violet loiters by the well,
And sweet to hear the shepherd Daphnis sing
    The song of Linus through a sunny dell
Of warm Arcadia where the corn is gold
And the slight lithe-limbed reapers dance about the wattled fold.

60

And sweet with young Lycoris to recline
  In some Illyrian valley far away,
Where canopied on herbs amaracine
  We too might waste the summer-trancèd day
Matching our reeds in sportive rivalry,
While far beneath us frets the troubled purple of the sea.

But sweeter far if silver-sandalled foot
  Of some long-hidden God should ever tread
The Nuneham meadows, if with reeded flute
  Pressed to his lips some Faun might raise his head   70
By the green water-flags, ah! sweet indeed
To see the heavenly herdsman call his white-fleeced flock to feed.

Then sing to me thou tuneful chorister,
  Though what thou sings't be thine own requiem!
Tell me thy tale thou hapless chronicler
  Of thine own tragedies! do not contemn
These unfamiliar haunts, this English field,
For many a lovely coronal our northern isle can yield

Which Grecian meadows know not, many a rose
  Which all day long in vales Æolian   80
A lad might seek in vain for overgrows
  Our hedges like a wanton courtezan
Unthrifty of its beauty, lilies too
Ilissus never mirrored star our streams, and cockles blue

Dot the green wheat which, though they are the signs
  For swallows going south, would never spread
Their azure tents between the Attic vines;
  Even that little weed of ragged red,
Which bids the robin pipe, in Arcady
Would be a trespasser, and many an unsung elegy   90

Sleeps in the reeds that fringe our winding Thames
  Which to awake were sweeter ravishment
Than ever Syrinx wept for, diadems
  Of brown bee-studded orchids which were meant
For Cytheræa's brows are hidden here
Unknown to Cytheræa, and by yonder pasturing steer

There is a tiny yellow daffodil,
    The butterfly can see it from afar,
Although one summer evening's dew could fill
    Its little cup twice over ere the star   100
Had called the lazy shepherd to his fold
And be no prodigal, each leaf is flecked with spotted gold

As if Jove's gorgeous leman Danae
    Hot from his gilded arms had stooped to kiss
The trembling petals, or young Mercury
    Low-flying to the dusky ford of Dis
Had with one feather of his pinions
Just brushed them! the slight stem which bears the burden of its
    suns

Is hardly thicker than the gossamer,
    Or poor Arachne's silver tapestry,—   110
Men say it bloomed upon the sepulchre
    Of One I sometime worshipped, but to me
It seems to bring diviner memories
Of faun-loved Heliconian glades and blue nymph-haunted seas,

Of an untrodden vale at Tempe where
    On the clear river's marge Narcissus lies,
The tangle of the forest in his hair,
    The silence of the woodland in his eyes,
Wooing that drifting imagery which is
No sooner kissed than broken, memories of Salmacis   120

Who is not boy or girl and yet is both,
    Fed by two fires and unsatisfied
Through their excess, each passion being loth
    For love's own sake to leave the other's side
Yet killing love by staying, memories
Of Oreads peeping through the leaves of silent moon-lit trees,

Of lonely Ariadne on the wharf
    At Naxos, when she saw the treacherous crew
Far out at sea, and waved her crimson scarf

And called false Theseus back again nor knew   130
That Dionysos on an amber pard
Was close behind her, memories of what Maeonia's bard

With sightless eyes beheld, the wall of Troy,
   Queen Helen lying in the ivory room,
And at her side an amorous red-lipped boy
   Trimming with dainty hand his helmet's plume,
And far away the moil, the shout, the groan,
As Hector shielded off the spear and Ajax hurled the stone;

Of wingèd Perseus with his flawless sword
   Cleaving the snaky tresses of the witch,   140
And all those tales imperishably stored
   In little Grecian urns, freightage more rich
Than any gaudy galleon of Spain
Bare from the Indies ever! these at least bring back again,

For well I know they are not dead at all,
   The ancient Gods of Grecian poesy,
They are asleep, and when they hear thee call
   Will wake and think 'tis very Thessaly,
This Thames the Daulian waters, this cool glade
The yellow-irised mead where once young Itys laughed and
   played.   150

If it was thou dear jasmine-cradled bird
   Who from the leafy stillness of thy throne
Sang to the wondrous boy, until he heard
   The horn of Atalanta faintly blown
Across the Cumnor hills, and wandering
Through Bagley wood at evening found the Attic poets' spring,—

Ah! tiny sober-suited advocate
   That pleadest for the moon against the day!
If thou didst make the shepherd seek his mate
   On that sweet questing, when Proserpina   160
Forgot it was not Sicily and leant
Across the mossy Sandford stile in ravished wonderment,—

Light-winged and bright-eyed miracle of the wood!
  If ever thou didst soothe with melody
One of that little clan, that brotherhood
  Which loved the morning-star of Tuscany
More than the perfect sun of Raphael
And is immortal, sing to me! for I too love thee well,

Sing on! sing on! let the dull world grow young,
  Let elemental things take form again,   170
And the old shapes of Beauty walk among
  The simple garths and open crofts, as when
The son of Leto bare the willow rod,
And the soft sheep and shaggy goats followed the boyish God.

Sing on! sing on! and Bacchus will be here
  Astride upon his gorgeous Indian throne,
And over whimpering tigers shake the spear
  With yellow ivy crowned and gummy cone,
While at his side the wanton Bassarid
Will throw the lion by the mane and catch the mountain kid! 180

Sing on! and I will wear the leopard skin,
  And steal the moonéd wings of Ashtaroth,
Upon whose icy chariot we could win
  Cithæron in an hour e'er the froth
Has overbrimmed the wine-vat or the Faun
Ceased from the treading! ay, before the flickering lamp of dawn

Has scared the hooting owlet to its nest,
  And warned the bat to close its filmy vans,
Some Mænad girl with vine-leaves on her breast
  Will filch their beechnuts from the sleeping Pans   190
So softly that the little nested thrush
Will never wake, and then with shrilly laugh and leap will rush

Down the green valley where the fallen dew
  Lies thick beneath the elm and count her store,
Till the brown Satyrs in a jolly crew
  Trample the loosestrife down along the shore,
And where their hornèd master sits in state
Bring strawberries and bloomy plums upon a wicker crate!

Sing on! and soon with passion-wearied face
　　Through the cool leaves Apollo's lad will come,   200
The Tyrian prince his bristled boar will chase
　　Adown the chestnut-copses all a-bloom,
And ivory-limbed, grey-eyed, with look of pride,
After yon velvet-coated deer the virgin maid will ride.

Sing on! and I the dying boy will see
　　Stain with his purple blood the waxen bell
That overweighs the jacinth, and to me
　　The wretched Cyprian her woe will tell,
And I will kiss her mouth and streaming eyes,
And lead her to the myrtle-hidden grove where Adon lies!   210

Cry out aloud on Itys! memory
　　That foster-brother of remorse and pain
Drops poison in mine ear,—O to be free,
　　To burn one's old ships! and to launch again
Into the white-plumed battle of the waves
And fight old Proteus for the spoil of coral-flowered caves!

O for Medea with her poppied spell!
　　O for the secret of the Colchian shrine!
O for one leaf of that pale asphodel
　　Which binds the tired brows of Proserpine,   220
And sheds such wondrous dews at eve that she
Dreams of the fields of Enna, by the far Sicilian sea,

Where oft the golden-girdled bee she chased
　　From lily to lily on the level mead,
Ere yet her sombre Lord had bid her taste
　　The deadly fruit of that pomegranate seed,
Ere the black steeds had harried her away
Down to the faint and flowerless land, the sick and sunless day.

O for one midnight and as paramour
　　The Venus of the little Melian farm!   230
O that some antique statue for one hour
　　Might wake to passion, and that I could charm
The Dawn at Florence from its dumb despair
Mix with those mighty limbs and make that giant breast my lair!

Sing on! sing on! I would be drunk with life,
  Drunk with the trampled vintage of my youth,
I would forget the wearying wasted strife,
  The riven veil, the Gorgon eyes of Truth,
The prayerless vigil and the cry for prayer,
The barren gifts, the lifted arms, the dull insensate air!   240

Sing on! sing on! O feathered Niobe,
  Thou canst make sorrow beautiful, and steal
From joy its sweetest music, not as we
  Who by dead voiceless silence strive to heal
Our too untented wounds, and do but keep
Pain barricadoed in our hearts, and murder pillowed sleep.

Sing louder yet, why must I still behold
  The wan white face of that deserted Christ,
Whose bleeding hands my hands did once enfold,
  Whose smitten lips my lips so oft have kissed,   250
And now in mute and marble misery
Sits in his lone dishonoured House and weeps, perchance for me.

O Memory cast down thy wreathèd shell!
  Break thy hoarse lute O sad Melpomene!
O Sorrow Sorrow keep thy cloistered cell
  Nor dim with tears this limpid Castaly!
Cease, Philomel, thou dost the forest wrong
To vex its sylvan quiet with such wild impassioned song!

Cease, cease, or if 'tis anguish to be dumb
  Take from the pastoral thrush her simpler air,   260
Whose jocund carelessness doth more become
  This English woodland than thy keen despair,
Ah! cease and let the north wind bear thy lay
Back to the rocky hills of Thrace, the stormy Daulian bay.

A moment more, the startled leaves had stirred,
  Endymion would have passed across the mead
Moonstruck with love, and this still Thames had heard
  Pan plash and paddle groping for some reed
To lure from her blue cave that Naiad maid
Who for such piping listens half in joy and half afraid.   270

A moment more, the waking dove had cooed,
  The silver daughter of the silver sea
With the fond gyves of clinging hands had wooed
  Her wanton from the chase, and Dryope
Had thrust aside the branches of her oak
To see the lusty gold-haired lad rein in his snorting yoke.

A moment more, the trees had stooped to kiss
  Pale Daphne just awakening from the swoon
Of tremulous laurels, lonely Salmacis
  Had bared his barren beauty to the moon,   280
And through the vale with sad voluptuous smile
Antinous had wandered, the red lotus of the Nile

Down leaning from his black and clustering hair,
  To shade those slumberous eyelids' caverned bliss,
Or else on yonder grassy slope with bare
  High-tuniced limbs unravished Artemis
Had bade her hounds give tongue, and roused the deer
From his green ambuscade with shrill halloo and pricking spear.

Lie still, lie still, O passionate heart, lie still!
  O Melancholy, fold thy raven wing!   290
O sobbing Dryad, from thy hollow hill
  Come not with such desponded answering!
No more thou wingèd Marsyas complain,
Apollo loveth not to hear such troubled songs of pain!

It was a dream, the glade is tenantless,
  No soft Ionian laughter moves the air,
The Thames creeps on in sluggish leadenness,
  And from the copse left desolate and bare
Fled is young Bacchus with his revelry,   299
Yet still from Nuneham wood there comes that thrilling melody

So sad, that one might think a human heart
  Brake in each separate note, a quality
Which music sometime has, being the Art

Which is most nigh to tears and memory,
Poor mourning Philomel, what dost thou fear?
Thy sister doth not haunt these fields, Pandion is not here,

Here is no cruel Lord with murderous blade,
    No woven web of bloody heraldries,
But mossy dells for roving comrades made,
    Warm valleys where the tired student lies   310
With half-shut book, and many a winding walk
Where rustic lovers stray at eve in happy simple talk.

The harmless rabbit gambols with its young
    Across the trampled towing-path, where late
A troop of laughing boys in jostling throng
    Cheered with their noisy cries the racing eight;
The gossamer, with ravelled silver threads,
Works at its little loom, and from the dusky red-eaved sheds

Of the lone Farm a flickering light shines out
    Where the swinked shepherd drives his bleating flock   320
Back to their wattled sheep-cotes, a faint shout
    Comes from some Oxford boat at Sandford lock,
And starts the moor-hen from the sedgy rill,
And the dim lengthening shadows flit like swallows up the hill.

The heron passes homeward to the mere,
    The blue mist creeps among the shivering trees,
Gold world by world the silent stars appear,
    And like a blossom blown before the breeze
A white moon drifts across the shimmering sky,
Mute arbitress of all thy sad, thy rapturous threnody.   330

She does not heed thee, wherefore should she heed,
    She knows Endymion is not far away,
'Tis I, 'tis I, whose soul is as the reed
    Which has no message of its own to play,
So pipes another's bidding, it is I,
Drifting with every wind on the wide sea of misery.

Ah! the brown bird has ceased: one exquisite trill
  About the sombre woodland seems to cling
Dying in music, else the air is still,
  So still that one might hear the bat's small wing   340
Wander and wheel above the pines, or tell
Each tiny dewdrop dripping from the blue-bell's brimming cell.

And far away across the lengthening wold,
  Across the willowy flats and thickets brown,
Magdalen's tall tower tipped with tremulous gold
  Marks the long High Street of the little town,
And warns me to return; I must not wait,
Hark! 'tis the curfew booming from the bell at Christ Church gate.

Theocritus: A Villanelle

O Singer of Persephone!
  In the dim meadows desolate
Dost thou remember Sicily?

Still through the ivy flits the bee
  Where Amaryllis lies in state;
O Singer of Persephone!

Simætha calls on Hecate
  And hears the wild dogs at the gate;
Dost thou remember Sicily?

Still by the light and laughing sea   10
  Poor Polypheme bemoans his fate:
O Singer of Persephone!

And still in boyish rivalry
  Young Daphnis challenges his mate:
Dost thou remember Sicily?

Slim Lacon keeps a goat for thee,
   For thee the jocund shepherds wait,
O Singer of Persephone!
Dost thou remember Sicily?

Endymion

(For Music)

The apple trees are hung with gold,
   And birds are loud in Arcady,
The sheep lie bleating in the fold,
The wild goat runs across the wold,
But yesterday his love he told,
   I know he will come back to me.
O rising moon! O Lady moon!
   Be you my lover's sentinel,
   You cannot choose but know him well,
For he is shod with purple shoon,   10
You cannot choose but know my love,
   For he a shepherd's crook doth bear,
And he is soft as any dove,
   And brown and curly is his hair.

The turtle now has ceased to call
   Upon her crimson-footed groom,
The grey wolf prowls about the stall,
The lily's singing seneschal
Sleeps in the lily-bell, and all
   The violet hills are lost in gloom.   20
O risen moon! O holy moon!
   Stand on the top of Helice,
   And if my own true love you see,
Ah! if you see the purple shoon,
The hazel crook, the lad's brown hair,
   The goat-skin wrapped about his arm,
Tell him that I am waiting where
   The rushlight glimmers in the Farm.

The falling dew is cold and chill,
    And no bird sings in Arcady,   30
The little fauns have left the hill,
Even the tired daffodil
Has closed its gilded doors, and still
    My lover comes not back to me.
False moon! False moon! O waning moon!
    Where is my own true lover gone,
    Where are the lips vermilion,
The shepherd's crook, the purple shoon?
Why spread that silver pavilion,
    Why wear that veil of drifting mist?   40
Ah! thou hast young Endymion,
    Thou hast the lips that should be kissed!

Charmides

He was a Grecian lad, who coming home
    With pulpy figs and wine from Sicily
Stood at his galley's prow, and let the foam
    Blow through his crisp brown curls unconsciously,
And holding wave and wind in boy's despite
Peered from his dripping seat across the wet and stormy night

Till with the dawn he saw a burnished spear
    Like a thin thread of gold against the sky,
And hoisted sail, and strained the creaking gear,
    And bade the pilot head her lustily   10
Against the nor'west gale, and all day long
Held on his way, and marked the rowers' time with measured song,

And when the faint Corinthian hills were red
    Dropped anchor in a little sandy bay,
And with fresh boughs of olive crowned his head,
    And brushed from cheek and throat the hoary spray,
And washed his limbs with oil, and from the hold
Brought out his linen tunic and his sandals brazen-soled,

And a rich robe stained with the fishes' juice
   Which of some swarthy trader he had bought   20
Upon the sunny quay at Syracuse,
   And was with Tyrian broideries inwrought,
And by the questioning merchants made his way
Up through the soft and silver woods, and when the labouring day

Had spun its tangled web of crimson cloud,
   Clomb the high hill, and with swift silent feet
Crept to the fane unnoticed by the crowd
   Of busy priests, and from some dark retreat
Watched the young swains his frolic playmates bring
The firstling of their little flock, and the shy shepherd fling   30

The crackling salt upon the flame, or hang
   His studded crook against the temple wall
To Her who keeps away the ravenous fang
   Of the base wolf from homestead and from stall;
And then the clear-voiced maidens 'gan to sing,
And to the altar each man brought some goodly offering,

A beechen cup brimming with milky foam,
   A fair cloth wrought with cunning imagery
Of hounds in chase, a waxen honey-comb
   Dripping with oozy gold which scarce the bee   40
Had ceased from building, a black skin of oil
Meet for the wrestlers, a great boar the fierce and white-tusked
    spoil

Stolen from Artemis that jealous maid
   To please Athena, and the dappled hide
Of a tall stag who in some mountain glade
   Had met the shaft; and then the herald cried,
And from the pillared precinct one by one
Went the glad Greeks well pleased that they their simple vows had
    done.

And the old priest put out the waning fires
   Save that one lamp whose restless ruby glowed   50
For ever in the cell, and the shrill lyres

Came fainter on the wind, as down the road
In joyous dance these country folk did pass,
And with stout hands the warder closed the gates of polished brass.

Long time he lay and hardly dared to breathe,
  And heard the cadenced drip of spilt-out wine,
And the rose-petals falling from the wreath
  As the night breezes wandered through the shrine,
And seemed to be in some entrancèd swoon
Till through the open roof above the full and brimming moon 60

Flooded with sheeny waves the marble floor,
  When from his nook upleapt the venturous lad,
And flinging wide the cedar-carven door
  Beheld an awful image saffron-clad
And armed for battle! the gaunt Griffin glared
From the huge helm, and the long lance of wreck and ruin flared

Like a red rod of flame, stony and steeled
  The Gorgon's head its leaden eyeballs rolled,
And writhed its snaky horrors through the shield,
  And gaped aghast with bloodless lips and cold   70
In passion impotent, while with blind gaze
The blinking owl between the feet hooted in shrill amaze.

The lonely fisher as he trimmed his lamp
  Far out at sea off Sunium, or cast
The net for tunnies, heard a brazen tramp
  Of horses smite the waves, and a wild blast
Divide the folded curtains of the night,
And knelt upon the little poop, and prayed in holy fright.

And guilty lovers in their venery
  Forgat a little while their stolen sweets,   80
Deeming they heard dread Dian's bitter cry;
  And the grim watchmen on their lofty seats
Ran to their shields in haste precipitate,
Or strained black-bearded throats across the dusky parapet.

For round the temple rolled the clang of arms,
   And the twelve Gods leapt up in marble fear,
And the air quaked with dissonant alarums
   Till huge Poseidon shook his mighty spear,
And on the frieze the prancing horses neighed,
And the low tread of hurrying feet rang from the cavalcade.   90

Ready for death with parted lips he stood,
   And well content at such a price to see
That calm wide brow, that terrible maidenhood,
   The marvel of that pitiless chastity,
Ah! well content indeed, for never wight
Since Troy's young shepherd prince had seen so wonderful a sight.

Ready for death he stood, but lo! the air
   Grew silent, and the horses ceased to neigh,
And off his brow he tossed the clustering hair,
   And from his limbs he threw the cloak away,   100
For whom would not such love make desperate,
And nigher came, and touched her throat, and with hands violate

Undid the cuirass, and the crocus gown,
   And bared the breasts of polished ivory,
Till from the waist the peplos falling down
   Left visible the secret mystery
Which to no lover will Athena show,
The grand cool flanks, the crescent thighs, the bossy hills of snow.

A little space he let his greedy eyes
   Rest on the burnished image, till mere sight   110
Half swooned for surfeit of such luxuries,
   And then his lips in hungering delight
Fed on her lips, and round the towered neck
He flung his arms, nor cared at all his passion's will to check.

Never I ween did lover hold such tryst,
   For all night long he murmured honeyed word,
And saw her sweet unravished limbs, and kissed
   Her pale and argent body undisturbed,
And paddled with the polished throat, and pressed
His hot and beating heart upon her chill and icy breast.   120

It was as if Numidian javelins
  Pierced through and through his wild and whirling brain,
And his nerves thrilled like throbbing violins
  In exquisite pulsation, and the pain
Was such sweet anguish that he never drew
His lips from hers till overhead the lark of warning flew.

The moon was girdled with a crystal rim,
  The sign which shipmen say is ominous
Of wrath in heaven, the wan stars were dim,
  And the low lightening east was tremulous   130
With the faint fluttering wings of flying dawn,
Ere from the silent sombre shrine this lover had withdrawn.

Down the steep rock with hurried feet and fast
  Clomb the brave lad, and reached the cave of Pan,
And heard the goat-foot snoring as he passed,
  And leapt upon a grassy knoll and ran
Like a young fawn unto an olive wood
Which in a shady valley by the well-built city stood.

And sought a little stream, which well he knew,
  For oftentimes with boyish careless shout   140
The green and crested grebe he would pursue,
  Or snare in woven net the silver trout,
And down amid the startled reeds he lay
Panting in breathless sweet affright, and waited for the day.

On the green bank he lay, and let one hand
  Dip in the cool dark eddies listlessly,
And soon the breath of morning came and fanned
  His hot flushed cheeks, or lifted wantonly
The tangled curls from off his forehead, while
He on the running water gazed with strange and secret smile. 150

And soon the shepherd in rough woollen cloak
  With his long crook undid the wattled cotes,
And from the stack a thin blue wreath of smoke
  Curled through the air across the ripening oats,
And on the hill the yellow house-dog bayed
As through the crisp and rustling fern the heavy cattle strayed.

And when the light-foot mower went afield
  Across the meadows laced with threaded dew,
And the sheep bleated on the misty weald,
  And from its nest the waking corn-crake flew,   160
Some woodmen saw him lying by the stream
And marvelled much that any lad so beautiful could seem,

Nor deemed him born of mortals, and one said,
  'It is young Hylas, that false runaway
Who with a Naiad now would make his bed
  Forgetting Herakles,' but others, 'Nay,
It is Narcissus, his own paramour,
Those are the fond and crimson lips no woman can allure.'

And when they nearer came a third one cried,
  'It is young Dionysos who has hid   170
His spear and fawnskin by the river side
  Weary of hunting with the Bassarid,
And wise indeed were we away to fly
They live not long who on the gods immortal come to spy.'

So turned they back, and feared to look behind,
  And told the timid swain how they had seen
Amid the reeds some woodland God reclined,
  And no man dared to cross the open green,
And on that day no olive-tree was slain,
Nor rushes cut, but all deserted was the fair domain.   180

Save when the neat-herd's lad, his empty pail
  Well slung upon his back, with leap and bound
Raced on the other side, and stopped to hail
  Hoping that he some comrade new had found,
And gat no answer, and then half afraid
Passed on his simple way, or down the still and silent glade

A little girl ran laughing from the farm
  Not thinking of love's secret mysteries,
And when she saw the white and gleaming arm
  And all his manlihood, with longing eyes   190
Whose passion mocked her sweet virginity
Watched him a-while, and then stole back sadly and wearily.

Far off he heard the city's hum and noise,
    And now and then the shriller laughter where
The passionate purity of brown-limbed boys
    Wrestled or raced in the clear healthful air,
And now and then a little tinkling bell
As the shorn wether led the sheep down to the mossy well.

Through the grey willows danced the fretful gnat,
    The grasshopper chirped idly from the tree,   200
In sleek and oily coat the water-rat
    Breasting the little ripples manfully
Made for the wild-duck's nest, from bough to bough
Hopped the shy finch, and the huge tortoise crept across the
    slough.

On the faint wind floated the silky seeds
    As the bright scythe swept through the waving grass,
The ousel-cock splashed circles in the reeds
    And flecked with silver whorls the forest's glass,
Which scarce had caught again its imagery
Ere from its bed the dusky tench leapt at the dragon-fly.   210

But little care had he for any thing
    Though up and down the beech the squirrel played,
And from the copse the linnet 'gan to sing
    To her brown mate her sweetest serenade,
Ah! little care indeed, for he had seen
The breasts of Pallas and the naked wonder of the Queen.

But when the herdsman called his straggling goats
    With whistling pipe across the rocky road,
And the shard-beetle with its trumpet-notes
    Boomed through the darkening woods, and seemed to bode   220
Of coming storm, and the belated crane
Passed homeward like a shadow, and the dull big drops of rain

Fell on the pattering fig-leaves, up he rose,
    And from the gloomy forest went his way
Past sombre homestead and wet orchard-close,

And came at last unto a little quay,
And called his mates a-board, and took his seat
On the high poop, and pushed from land, and loosed the dripping
    sheet,

And steered across the bay, and when nine suns
    Passed down the long and laddered way of gold,   230
And nine pale moons had breathed their orisons
    To the chaste stars their confessors, or told
Their dearest secret to the downy moth
That will not fly at noonday, through the foam and surging froth

Came a great owl with yellow sulphurous eyes
    And lit upon the ship, whose timbers creaked
As though the lading of three argosies
    Were in the hold, and flapped its wings, and shrieked,
And darkness straightway stole across the deep,
Sheathed was Orion's sword, dread Mars himself fled down the
    steep,   240

And the moon hid behind a tawny mask
    Of drifting cloud, and from the ocean's marge
Rose the red plume, the huge and hornèd casque,
    The seven-cubit spear, the brazen targe!
And clad in bright and burnished panoply
Athena strode across the stretch of sick and shivering sea!

To the dull sailors' sight her loosened locks
    Seemed like the jagged storm-rack, and her feet
Only the spume that floats on hidden rocks,
    And, marking how the rising waters beat   250
Against the rolling ship, the pilot cried
To the young helmsman at the stern to luff to windward side.

But he, the over-bold adulterer,
    A dear profaner of great mysteries,
An ardent amorous idolater,
    When he beheld those grand relentless eyes
Laughed loud for joy, and crying out 'I come'
Leapt from the lofty poop into the chill and churning foam.

Then fell from the high heaven one bright star,
   One dancer left the circling galaxy,   260
And back to Athens on her clattering car
   In all the pride of venged divinity
Pale Pallas swept with shrill and steely clank,
And a few gurgling bubbles rose where her boy lover sank.

And the mast shuddered as the gaunt owl flew
   With mocking hoots after the wrathful Queen,
And the old pilot bade the trembling crew
   Hoist the big sail, and told how he had seen
Close to the stern a dim and giant form,
And like a dipping swallow the stout ship dashed through the
     storm.   270

And no man dared to speak of Charmides
   Deeming that he some evil thing had wrought,
And when they reached the strait Symplegades
   They beached their galley on the shore, and sought
The toll-gate of the city hastily,
And in the market showed their brown and pictured pottery.

II

But some good Triton-god had ruth, and bare
   The boy's drowned body back to Grecian land,
And mermaids combed his dank and dripping hair
   And smoothed his brow, and loosed his clenching hand,   280
Some brought sweet spices from far Araby,
And others bade the halcyon sing her softest lullaby.

And when he neared his old Athenian home,
   A mighty billow rose up suddenly
Upon whose oily back the clotted foam
   Lay diapered in some strange fantasy,
And clasping him unto its glassy breast,
Swept landward, like a white-maned steed upon a venturous quest!

Now where Colonos leans unto the sea
    There lies a long and level stretch of lawn,   290
The rabbit knows it, and the mountain bee
    For it deserts Hymettus, and the Faun
Is not afraid, for never through the day
Comes a cry ruder than the shout of shepherd lads at play.

But often from the thorny labyrinth
    And tangled branches of the circling wood
The stealthy hunter sees young Hyacinth
    Hurling the polished disk, and draws his hood
Over his guilty gaze, and creeps away,
Nor dares to wind his horn, or—else at the first break of day 300

The Dryads come and throw the leathern ball
    Along the reedy shore, and circumvent
Some goat-eared Pan to be their seneschal
    For fear of bold Poseidon's ravishment,
And loose their girdles, with shy timorous eyes,
Lest from the surf his azure arms and purple beard should rise.

On this side and on that a rocky cave,
    Hung with the yellow-bell'd laburnum, stands,
Smooth is the beach, save where some ebbing wave
    Leaves its faint outline etched upon the sands,   310
As though it feared to be too soon forgot
By the green rush, its playfellow,—and yet, it is a spot

So small, that the inconstant butterfly
    Could steal the hoarded honey from each flower
Ere it was noon, and still not satisfy
    Its over-greedy love,—within an hour
A sailor boy, were he but rude enow
To land and pluck a garland for his galley's painted prow,

Would almost leave the little meadow bare,
    For it knows nothing of great pageantry,   320
Only a few narcissi here and there
    Stand separate in sweet austerity,
Dotting the unmown grass with silver stars,
And here and there a daffodil waves tiny scimetars.

Hither the billow brought him, and was glad
  Of such dear servitude, and where the land
Was virgin of all waters laid the lad
  Upon the golden margent of the strand,
And like a lingering lover oft returned   229
To kiss those pallid limbs which once with intense fire burned,

Ere the wet seas had quenched that holocaust,
  That self-fed flame, that passionate lustihead,
Ere grisly death with chill and nipping frost
  Had withered up those lilies white and red
Which, while the boy would through the forest range,
Answered each other in a sweet antiphonal counter-change.

And when at dawn the woodnymphs, hand-in-hand,
  Threaded the bosky dell, their satyr spied
The boy's pale body stretched upon the sand,
  And feared Poseidon's treachery, and cried,   340
And like bright sunbeams flitting through a glade,
Each startled Dryad sought some safe and leafy ambuscade.

Save one white girl, who deemed it would not be
  So dread a thing to feel a sea-god's arms
Crushing her breasts in amorous tyranny,
  And longed to listen to those subtle charms
Insidious lovers weave when they would win
Some fencèd fortress, and stole back again, nor thought it sin

To yield her treasure unto one so fair,
  And lay beside him, thirsty with love's drouth,   350
Called him soft names, played with his tangled hair,
  And with hot lips made havoc of his mouth
Afraid he might not wake, and then afraid
Lest he might wake too soon, fled back, and then, fond renegade,

Returned to fresh assault, and all day long
  Sat at his side, and laughed at her new toy,
And held his hand, and sang her sweetest song,

Then frowned to see how froward was the boy
Who would not with her maidenhood entwine,   359
Nor knew that three days since his eyes had looked on Proserpine,

Nor knew what sacrilege his lips had done,
   But said, 'He will awake, I know him well,
He will awake at evening when the sun
   Hangs his red shield on Corinth's citadel,
This sleep is but a cruel treachery
To make me love him more, and in some cavern of the sea

Deeper than ever falls the fisher's line
   Already a huge Triton blows his horn,
And weaves a garland from the crystalline
   And drifting ocean-tendrils to adorn   370
The emerald pillars of our bridal bed,
For sphered in foaming silver, and with coral-crownèd head,

We two will sit upon a throne of pearl,
   And a blue wave will be our canopy,
And at our feet the water-snakes will curl
   In all their amethystine panoply
Of diamonded mail, and we will mark
The mullets swimming by the mast of some storm-foundered bark,

Vermilion-finned with eyes of bossy gold
   Like flakes of crimson light, and the great deep   380
His glassy-portaled chamber will unfold,
   And we will see the painted dolphins sleep
Cradled by murmuring halcyons on the rocks
Where Proteus in quaint suit of green pastures his monstrous
   flocks.

And tremulous opal-hued anemones
   Will wave their purple fringes where we tread
Upon the mirrored floor, and argosies
   Of fishes flecked with tawny scales will thread
The drifting cordage of the shattered wreck,
And honey-coloured amber beads our twining limbs will deck.'

                                                              390

But when that baffled Lord of War the Sun
   With gaudy pennon flying passed away
Into his brazen House, and one by one
   The little yellow stars began to stray
Across the field of heaven, ah! then indeed
She feared his lips upon her lips would never care to feed,

And cried, 'Awake, already the pale moon
   Washes the trees with silver, and the wave
Creeps grey and chilly up this sandy dune,
   The croaking frogs are out, and from the cave   400
The night-jar shrieks, the fluttering bats repass,
And the brown stoat with hollow flanks creeps through the dusky
    grass.

Nay, though thou art a God, be not so coy,
   For in yon stream there is a little reed
That often whispers how a lovely boy
   Lay with her once upon a grassy mead,
Who when his cruel pleasure he had done
Spread wings of rustling gold and soared aloft into the sun.

Be not so coy, the laurel trembles still
   With great Apollo's kisses, and the fir   410
Whose clustering sisters fringe the sea-ward hill
   Hath many a tale of that bold ravisher
Whom men call Boreas, and I have seen
The mocking eyes of Hermes through the poplar's silvery sheen.

Even the jealous Naiads call me fair,
   And every morn a young and ruddy swain
Woos me with apples and with locks of hair,
   And seeks to soothe my virginal disdain
By all the gifts the gentle wood-nymphs love;
But yesterday he brought to me an iris-plumaged dove   420

With little crimson feet, which with its store
   Of seven spotted eggs the cruel lad
Had stolen from the lofty sycamore

At day-break, when her amorous comrade had
Flown off in search of berried juniper
Which most they love; the fretful wasp, that earliest vintager

Of the blue grapes, hath not persistency
   So constant as this simple shepherd-boy
For my poor lips, his joyous purity
   And laughing sunny eyes might well decoy   430
A Dryad from her oath to Artemis;
For very beautiful is he, his mouth was made to kiss,

His argent forehead, like a rising moon
   Over the dusky hills of meeting brows,
Is crescent shaped, the hot and Tyrian noon
   Leads from the myrtle-grove no goodlier spouse
For Cytheræa, the first silky down
Fringes his blushing cheeks, and his young limbs are strong and
      brown:

And he is rich, and fat and fleecy herds
   Of bleating sheep upon his meadows lie,   440
And many an earthern bowl of yellow curds
   Is in his homestead for the thievish fly
To swim and drown in, the pink clover mead
Keeps its sweet store for him, and he can pipe on oaten reed.

And yet I love him not, it was for thee
   I kept my love, I knew that thou would'st come
To rid me of this pallid chastity;
   Thou fairest flower of the flowerless foam
Of all the wide Ægean, brightest star
Of ocean's azure heavens where the mirrored planets are!   450

I knew that thou would'st come, for when at first
   The dry wood burgeoned, and the sap of Spring
Swelled in my green and tender bark or burst
   To myriad multitudinous blossoming
Which mocked the midnight with its mimic moons
That did not dread the dawn, and first the thrushes' rapturous
      tunes

Startled the squirrel from its granary,
   And cuckoo flowers fringed the narrow lane,
Through my young leaves a sensuous ecstasy
   Crept like new wine, and every mossy vein   460
Throbbed with the fitful pulse of amorous blood,
And the wild winds of passion shook my slim stem's maidenhood.

The trooping fawns at evening came and laid
   Their cool black noses on my lowest boughs,
And on my topmost branch the blackbird made
   A little nest of grasses for his spouse,
And now and then a twittering wren would light
On a thin twig which hardly bare the weight of such delight.

I was the Attic shepherd's trysting place,
   Beneath my shadow Amaryllis lay,   470
And round my trunk would laughing Daphnis chase
   The timorous girl, till tired out with play
She felt his hot breath stir her tangled hair,
And turned, and looked, and fled no more from such delightful
    snare.

Then come away unto my ambuscade
   Where clustering woodbine weaves a canopy
For amorous pleasaunce, and the rustling shade
   Of Paphian myrtles seems to sanctify
The dearest rites of love, there in the cool
And green recesses of its farthest depth there is a pool,   480

The ouzel's haunt, the wild bee's pasturage,
   For round its rim great creamy lilies float
Through their flat leaves in verdant anchorage,
   Each cup a white-sailed golden-laden boat
Steered by a dragon-fly,—be not afraid
To leave this wan and wave-kissed shore, surely the place was made

For lovers such as we, the Cyprian Queen,
   One arm around her boyish paramour,
Strays often there at eve, and I have seen

The moon strip off her misty vestiture   490
For young Endymion's eyes, be not afraid,
The panther feet of Dian never tread that secret glade.

Nay if thou wil'st, back to the beating brine,
  Back to the boisterous billow let us go,
And walk all day beneath the hyaline
  Huge vault of Neptune's watery portico,
And watch the purple monsters of the deep
Sport in ungainly play, and from his lair keen Xiphias leap.

For if my mistress find me lying here
  She will not ruth or gentle pity show,   500
But lay her boar-spear down, and with austere
  Relentless fingers string the cornel bow,
And draw the feathered notch against her breast,
And loose the archèd cord, ay, even now upon the quest

I hear her hurrying feet,—awake, awake,
  Thou laggard in love's battle! once at least
Let me drink deep of passion's wine, and slake
  My parchèd being with the nectarous feast
Which even Gods affect! O come Love come,
Still we have time to reach the cavern of thine azure home.'   510

Scarce had she spoken when the shuddering trees
  Shook, and the leaves divided, and the air
Grew conscious of a God, and the grey seas
  Crawled backward, and a long and dismal blare
Blew from some tasselled horn, a sleuth-hound bayed,
And like a flame a barbèd reed flew whizzing down the glade.

And where the little flowers of her breast
  Just brake into their milky blossoming,
This murderous paramour, this unbidden guest,
  Pierced and struck deep in horrid chambering,   520
And ploughed a bloody furrow with its dart,
And dug a long red road, and cleft with wingèd death her heart.

Sobbing her life out with a bitter cry,
  On the boy's body fell the Dryad maid,
Sobbing for incomplete virginity,
  And raptures unenjoyed, and pleasures dead,
And all the pain of things unsatisfied,
And the bright drops of crimson youth crept down her throbbing
    side.

Ah! pitiful it was to hear her moan,
  And very pitiful to see her die   530
Ere she had yielded up her sweets, or known
  The joy of passion, that dread mystery
Which not to know is not to live at all,
And yet to know is to be held in death's most deadly thrall.

But as it hapt the Queen of Cythere,
  Who with Adonis all night long had lain
Within some shepherd's hut in Arcady,
  On team of silver doves and gilded wane
Was journeying Paphos-ward, high up afar
From mortal ken between the mountains and the morning star,

                                                                    540

And when low down she spied the hapless pair
  And heard the Oread's faint despairing cry,
Whose cadence seemed to play upon the air
  As though it were a viol, hastily
She bade her pigeons fold each straining plume,
And dropt to earth, and reached the strand, and saw their dolorous
    doom.

For as a gardener turning back his head
  To catch the last notes of the linnet mows
With careless scythe too near some flower bed,
  And cuts the thorny pillar of the rose,   550
And with the flower's loosened loveliness
Strews the brown mould, or as some shepherd lad in wantonness

Driving his little flock along the mead
  Treads down two daffodils which side by side
Have lured the lady-bird with yellow brede

And made the gaudy moth forget its pride,
Treads down their brimming golden chalices
Under light feet which were not made for such rude ravages,

Or as a schoolboy tired of his book
  Flings himself down upon the reedy grass   560
And plucks two water-lilies from the brook,
  And for a time forgets the hour glass,
Then wearies of their sweets, and goes his way,
And lets the hot sun kill them, even so these lovers lay.

And Venus cried, 'It is dread Artemis
  Whose bitter hand hath wrought this cruelty,
Or else that mightier may whose care it is
  To guard her strong and stainless majesty
Upon the hill Athenian,—alas!
That they who loved so well unloved into Death's house should
      pass.'   570

So with soft hands she laid the boy and girl
  In the great golden waggon tenderly,
Her white throat whiter than a moony pearl
  Just threaded with a blue vein's tapestry
Had not yet ceased to throb, and still her breast
Swayed like a wind-stirred lily in ambiguous unrest.

And then each pigeon spread its milky van,
  The bright car soared into the dawning sky,
And like a cloud the aerial caravan
  Passed over the Ægean silently,   580
Till the faint air was troubled with the song
From the wan mouths that call on bleeding Thammuz all night
      long.

But when the doves had reached their wonted goal
  Where the wide stair of orbèd marble dips
Its snows into the sea, her fluttering soul
  Just shook the trembling petals of her lips
And passed into the void, and Venus knew
That one fair maid the less would walk amid her retinue,

And bade her servants carve a cedar chest
  With all the wonder of this history,   590
Within whose scented womb their limbs should rest
  Where olive-trees make tender the blue sky
On the low hills of Paphos, and the faun
Pipes in the noonday, and the nightingale sings on till dawn.

Nor failed they to obey her hest, and ere
  The morning bee had stung the daffodil
With tiny fretful spear, or from its lair
  The waking stag had leapt across the rill
And roused the ouzel, or the lizard crept
Athwart the sunny rock, beneath the grass their bodies slept. 600

And when day brake, within that silver shrine
  Fed by the flames of cressets tremulous,
Queen Venus knelt and prayed to Proserpine
  That she whose beauty made Death amorous
Should beg a guerdon from her pallid Lord,
And let Desire pass across dread Charon's icy ford.

III

In melancholy moonless Acheron,
  Far from the goodly earth and joyous day,
Where no spring ever buds, nor ripening sun
  Weighs down the apple trees, nor flower May   610
Chequers with chestnut blooms the grassy floor,
Where thrushes never sing, and piping linnets mate no more,

There by a dim and dark Lethæan well
  Young Charmides was lying, wearily
He plucked the blossoms from the asphodel
  And with its little rifled treasury
Strewed the dull waters of the dusky stream,
And watched the white stars founder, and the land was like a
    dream.

When as he gazed into the watery glass
  And through his brown hair's curly tangles scanned   620
His own wan face, a shadow seemed to pass

Across the mirror, and a little hand
Stole into his, and warm lips timidly
Brushed his pale cheeks, and breathed their secret forth into a sigh.

Then turned he round his weary eyes and saw,
    And ever nigher still their faces came,
And nigher ever did their young mouths draw
    Until they seemed one perfect rose of flame,
And longing arms around her neck he cast,   629
And felt her throbbing bosom, and his breath came hot and fast,

And all his hoarded sweets were hers to kiss,
    And all her maidenhood was his to slay,
And limb to limb in long and rapturous bliss
    Their passion waxed and waned,—O why essay
To pipe again of love too venturous reed!
Enough, enough that Erôs laughed upon that flowerless mead.

Too venturous poesy O why essay
    To pipe again of passion! fold thy wings
O'er daring Icarus and bid thy lay
    Sleep hidden in the lyre's silent strings   640
Till thou hast found the old Castalian rill,
Or from the Lesbian waters plucked drowned Sappho's golden
    quill!

Enough, enough that he whose life had been
    A fiery pulse of sin, a splendid shame,
Could in the loveless land of Hades glean
    One scorching harvest from those fields of flame
Where passion walks with naked unshod feet
And is not wounded,—ah! enough that once their lips could meet

In that wild throb when all existences
    Seem narrowed to one single ecstasy   650
Which dies through its own sweetness and the stress
    Of too much pleasure, ere Persephone
Had bade them serve her by the ebon throne
Of the pale God who in the fields of Enna loosed her zone.

Ballade de Marguerite
(Normande)

I am weary of lying within the chase
When the knights are meeting in market-place.

Nay, go not thou to the red-roofed town
Lest the hooves of the war-horse tread thee down.

But I would not go where the Squires ride,
I would only walk by my Lady's side.

Alack! and alack! thou art over bold,
A Forester's son may not eat off gold.

Will she love me the less that my Father is seen
Each Martinmas day in a doublet green?   10

Perchance she is sewing at tapestrie,
Spindle and loom are not meet for thee.

Ah, if she is working the arras bright
I might ravel the threads by the fire-light.

Perchance she is hunting of the deer,
How could you follow o'er hill and meer?

Ah, if she is riding with the court,
I might run beside her and wind the morte.

Perchance she is kneeling in S. Denys,
(On her soul may our Lady have gramercy!)   20

Ah, if she is praying in lone chapelle,
I might swing the censer and ring the bell.

Come in, my son, for you look sae pale,
The father shall fill thee a stoup of ale.

But who are these knights in bright array?
Is it a pageant the rich folks play?

'Tis the King of England from over sea,
Who has come unto visit our fair countrie.

But why does the curfew toll sae low?
And why do the mourners walk a-row?   30

O 'tis Hugh of Amiens my sister's son
Who is lying stark, for his day is done.

Nay, nay, for I see white lilies clear,
It is no strong man who lies on the bier.

O 'tis old Dame Jeanette that kept the hall,
I knew she would die at the autumn fall.

Dame Jeanette had not that gold-brown hair,
Old Jeanette was not a maiden fair.

O 'tis none of our kith and none of our kin,
(Her soul may our Lady assoil from sin!)   40

But I hear the boy's voice chaunting sweet,
'Elle est morte, la Marguerite.'

Come in, my son, and lie on the bed,
And let the dead folk bury their dead.

O mother, you know I loved her true:
O mother, hath one grave room for two?

Humanitad

It is full Winter now: the trees are bare,
 Save where the cattle huddle from the cold
Beneath the pine, for it doth never wear

The Autumn's gaudy livery whose gold
Her jealous brother pilfers, but is true
To the green doublet; bitter is the wind, as though it blew

From Saturn's cave; a few thin wisps of hay
    Lie on the sharp black hedges, where the wain
Dragged the sweet pillage of a summer's day
    From the low meadows up the narrow lane;   10
Upon the half-thawed snow the bleating sheep
Press close against the hurdles, and the shivering house-dogs creep

From the shut stable to the frozen stream
    And back again disconsolate, and miss
The bawling shepherds and the noisy team;
    And overhead in circling listlessness
The cawing rooks whirl round the frosted stack,
Or crowd the dripping boughs; and in the fen the ice-pools crack

Where the gaunt bittern stalks among the reeds
    And flaps his wings, and stretches back his neck,   20
And hoots to see the moon; across the meads
    Limps the poor frightened hare, a little speck;
And a stray seamew with its fretful cry
Flits like a sudden drift of snow against the dull grey sky.

Full winter: and the lusty goodman brings
    His load of faggots from the chilly byre,
And stamps his feet upon the hearth, and flings
    The sappy billets on the waning fire,
And laughs to see the sudden lightening scare
His children at their play; and yet,—the Spring is in the air,   30

Already the slim crocus stirs the snow,
    And soon yon blanchèd fields will bloom again
With nodding cowslips for some lad to mow,
    For with the first warm kisses of the rain
The winter's icy sorrow breaks to tears,
And the brown thrushes mate, and with bright eyes the rabbit
    peers

From the dark warren where the fir-cones lie,
　　And treads one snowdrop under foot, and runs
Over the mossy knoll, and blackbirds fly
　　Across our path at evening, and the suns　　　　　　40
Stay longer with us; ah! how good to see
Grass-girdled Spring in all her joy of laughing greenery

Dance through the hedges till the early rose,
　　(That sweet repentance of the thorny briar!)
Burst from its sheathèd emerald and disclose
　　The little quivering disk of golden fire
Which the bees know so well, for with it come
Pale boys-love, sops-in-wine, and daffadillies all in bloom.

Then up and down the field the sower goes,
　　While close behind the laughing younker scares　　　50
With shrilly whoop the black and thievish crows,
　　And then the chestnut-tree its glory wears;
And on the grass the creamy blossom falls
In odorous excess, and faint half-whispered madrigals

Steal from the bluebells' nodding carillons
　　Each breezy morn, and then white jessamine,
That star of its own heaven, snapdragons
　　With lolling crimson tongues, and eglantine
In dusty velvets clad usurp the bed
And woodland empery, and when the lingering rose hath shed　60

Red leaf by leaf its folded panoply,
　　And pansies closed their purple-lidded eyes,
Chrysanthemums from gilded argosy
　　Unload their gaudy scentless merchandise,
And violets getting overbold withdraw
From their shy nooks, and scarlet berries dot the leafless haw.

O happy field! and O thrice happy tree!
　　Soon will your queen in daisy-flowered smock
And crown of flowre-de-luce trip down the lea,

Soon will the lazy shepherds drive their flock   70
Back to the pasture by the pool, and soon
Through the green leaves will float the hum of murmuring bees at
    noon.

Soon will the glade be bright with bellamour,
    The flower which wantons love, and those sweet nuns
Vale-lilies in their snowy vestiture
    Will tell their beaded pearls, and carnations
With mitred dusky leaves will scent the wind,
And straggling traveller's joy each hedge with yellow stars will
    bind.

Dear Bride of Nature and most bounteous Spring!
    That cans't give increase to the sweet-breath'd kine,   80
And to the kid its little horns, and bring
    The soft and silky blossoms to the vine,
Where is that old nepenthe which of yore
Man got from poppy root and glossy-berried mandragore!

There was a time when any common bird
    Could make me sing in unison, a time
When all the strings of boyish life were stirred
    To quick response or more melodious rhyme
By every forest idyll;—do I change?
Or rather doth some evil thing through thy fair pleasaunce range?
                                                        90

Nay, nay, thou art the same: 'tis I who seek
    To vex with sighs thy simple solitude,
And because fruitless tears bedew my cheek
    Would have thee weep with me in brotherhood;
Fool! shall each wronged and restless spirit dare
To taint such wine with the salt poison of his own despair!

Thou art the same: 'tis I whose wretched soul
    Takes discontent to be its paramour,
And gives its kingdom to the rude control
    Of what should be its servitor,—for sure   100
Wisdom is somewhere, though the stormy sea
Contain it not, and the huge deep answer ' 'Tis not in me.'

To burn with one clear flame, to stand erect
  In natural honour, not to bend the knee
In profitless prostrations whose effect
  Is by itself condemned, what alchemy
Can teach me this? what herb Medea brewed
Will bring the unexultant peace of essence not subdued?

The minor chord which ends the harmony,
  And for its answering brother waits in vain   110
Sobbing for incompleted melody,
  Dies a Swan's death; but I the heir of pain,
A silent Memnon with blank lidless eyes,
Wait for the light and music of those suns which never rise.

The quenched-out torch, the lonely cypress-gloom,
  The little dust stored in the narrow urn,
The gentle *XAIPE* of the Attic tomb,—
  Were not these better far than to return
To my old fitful restless malady,
Or spend my days within the voiceless cave of misery?   120

Nay! for perchance that poppy-crownèd God
  Is like the watcher by a sick man's bed
Who talks of sleep but gives it not; his rod
  Hath lost its virtue, and, when all is said,
Death is too rude, too obvious a key
To solve one single secret in a life's philosophy.

And Love! that noble madness, whose august
  And inextinguishable might can slay
The soul with honied drugs,—alas! I must
  From such sweet ruin play the runaway,   130
Although too constant memory never can
Forget the archèd splendour of those brows Olympian

Which for a little season made my youth
  So soft a swoon of exquisite indolence
That all the chiding of more prudent Truth
  Seemed the thin voice of jealousy,—O Hence
Thou huntress deadlier than Artemis!
Go seek some other quarry! for of thy too perilous bliss

My lips have drunk enough,—no more, no more,—
   Though Love himself should turn his gilded prow   140
Back to the troubled waters of this shore
   Where I am wrecked and stranded, even now
The Chariot wheels of passion sweep too near,
Hence! Hence! I pass unto a life more barren, more austere.

More barren—ay, those arms will never lean
   Down through the trellised vines and draw my soul
In sweet reluctance through the tangled green;
   Some other head must wear that aureole,
For I am Hers who loves not any man
Whose white and stainless bosom bears the sign Gorgonian.   150

Let Venus go and chuck her dainty page,
   And kiss his mouth, and toss his curly hair,
With net and spear and hunting equipage
   Let young Adonis to his tryst repair,
But me her fond and subtle-fashioned spell
Delights no more, though I could win her dearest citadel.

Ay, though I were that laughing shepherd boy
   Who from Mount Ida saw the little cloud
Pass over Tenedos and lofty Troy
   And knew the coming of the Queen, and bowed   160
In wonder at her feet, not for the sake
Of a new Helen would I bid her hand the apple take.

Then rise supreme Athena argent-limbed!
   And, if my lips be musicless, inspire
At least my life: was not thy glory hymned
   By One who gave to thee his sword and lyre
Like Æschylos at well-fought Marathon,
And died to show that Milton's England still could bear a son!

And yet I cannot tread the Portico
   And live without desire, fear, and pain,   170
Or nurture that wise calm which long ago
   The grave Athenian master taught to men,
Self-poised, self-centred, and self-comforted,
To watch the world's vain phantasies go by with unbowed head.

Alas! that serene brow, those eloquent lips,
　　Those eyes that mirrored all eternity,
Rest in their own Colonos, an eclipse
　　Hath come on Wisdom, and Mnemosyne
Is childless; in the night which she had made
For lofty secure flight Athena's owl itself hath strayed.　　　　180

Nor much with Science do I care to climb,
　　Although by strange and subtle witchery
She draw the moon from heaven: the Muse of Time
　　Unrolls her gorgeous-coloured tapestry
To no less eager eyes; often indeed
In the great epic of Polymnia's scroll I love to read

How Asia sent her myriad hosts to war
　　Against a little town, and panoplied
In gilded mail with jewelled scimetar,
　　White-shielded, purple-crested, rode the Mede　　　　190
Between the waving poplars and the sea
Which men call Artemisium, till he saw Thermopylæ

Its steep ravine spanned by a narrow wall,
　　And on the nearer side a little brood
Of careless lions holding festival!
　　And stood amazèd at such hardihood,
And pitched his tent upon the reedy shore,
And stayed two days to wonder, and then crept at midnight o'er

Some unfrequented height, and coming down
　　The autumn forests treacherously slew　　　　200
What Sparta held most dear and was the crown
　　Of far Eurotas, and passed on, nor knew
How God had staked an evil net for him
In the small bay at Salamis,—and yet, the page grows dim,

Its cadenced Greek delights me not, I feel
　　With such a goodly time too out of tune
To love it much: for like the Dial's wheel
　　That from its blinded darkness strikes the noon
Yet never sees the sun, so do my eyes
Restlessly follow that which from my cheated vision flies.　　　　210

O for one grand unselfish simple life
  To teach us what is Wisdom! speak ye hills
Of lone Helvellyn, for this note of strife
  Shunned your untroubled crags and crystal rills,
Where is that Spirit which living blamelessly
Yet dared to kiss the smitten mouth of his own century!

Speak ye Rydalian laurels! where is He
  Whose gentle head ye sheltered, that pure soul
Whose gracious days of uncrowned majesty
  Through lowliest conduct touched the lofty goal   220
Where Love and Duty mingle! Him at least
The most high Laws were glad of, He had sat at Wisdom's feast,

But we are Learning's changelings, know by rote
  The clarion watchword of each Grecian school
And follow none, the flawless sword which smote
  The pagan Hydra is an effete tool
Which we ourselves have blunted, what man now
Shall scale the august ancient heights and to old Reverence bow?

One such indeed I saw, but, Ichabod!
  Gone is that last dear son of Italy,   230
Who being man died for the sake of God,
  And whose unrisen bones sleep peacefully,
O guard him, guard him well, my Giotto's tower,
Thou marble lily of the lily town! let not the lour

Of the rude tempest vex his slumber, or
  The Arno with its tawny troubled gold
O'erleap its marge, no mightier conqueror
  Clomb the high Capitol in the days of old
When Rome was indeed Rome, for Liberty
Walked like a Bride beside him, at which sight pale Mystery 240

Fled shrieking to her farthest sombrest cell
  With an old man who grabbled rusty keys,
Fled shuddering for that immemorial knell
  With which oblivion buries dynasties
Swept like a wounded eagle on the blast,
As to the holy heart of Rome the great triumvir passed.

He knew the holiest heart and heights of Rome,
  He drave the base wolf from the lion's lair,
And now lies dead by that empyreal dome
  Which overtops Valdarno hung in air   250
By Brunelleschi—O Melpomene
Breathe through thy melancholy pipe thy sweetest threnody!

Breathe through the tragic stops such melodies
  That Joy's self may grow jealous, and the Nine
Forget a-while their discreet emperies,
  Mourning for him who on Rome's lordliest shrine
Lit for men's lives the light of Marathon,
And bare to sun-forgotten fields the fire of the sun!

O guard him, guard him well, my Giotto's tower,
  Let some young Florentine each eventide   260
Bring coronals of that enchanted flower
  Which the dim woods of Vallombrosa hide,
And deck the marble tomb wherein he lies
Whose soul is as some mighty orb unseen of mortal eyes.

Some mighty orb whose cycled wanderings,
  Being tempest-driven to the farthest rim
Where Chaos meets Creation and the wings
  Of the eternal chanting Cherubim
Are pavilioned on Nothing, passed away   269
Into a moonless void,—and yet, though he is dust and clay,

He is not dead, the immemorial Fates
  Forbid it, and the closing shears refrain,
Lift up your heads ye everlasting gates!
  Ye argent clarions sound a loftier strain!
For the vile thing he hated lurks within
Its sombre house, alone with God and memories of sin.

Still what avails it that she sought her cave
  That murderous mother of red harlotries?
At Munich on the marble architrave

The Grecian boys die smiling, but the seas   280
Which wash Ægina fret in loneliness
Not mirroring their beauty, so our lives grow colourless

For lack of our ideals, if one star
    Flame torch-like in the heavens the unjust
Swift daylight kills it, and no trump of war
    Can wake to passionate voice the silent dust
Which was Mazzini once! rich Niobe
For all her stony sorrows hath her sons, but Italy!

What Easter Day shall make her children rise,
    Who were not Gods yet suffered? what sure feet   290
Shall find their graveclothes folded? what clear eyes
    Shall see them bodily? O it were meet
To roll the stone from off the sepulchre
And kiss the bleeding roses of their wounds, in love of Her

Our Italy! our mother visible!
    Most blessed among nations and most sad,
For whose dear sake the young Calabrian fell
    That day at Aspromonte and was glad
That in an age when God was bought and sold   299
One man could die for Liberty! but we, burnt out and cold,

See Honour smitten on the cheek and gyves
    Bind the sweet feet of Mercy: Poverty
Creeps through our sunless lanes and with sharp knives
    Cuts the warm throats of children stealthily,
And no word said: —O we are wretched men
Unworthy of our great inheritance! where is the pen

Of austere Milton? where the mighty sword
    Which slew its master righteously? the years
Have lost their ancient leader, and no word
    Breaks from the voiceless tripod on our ears: 310
While as a ruined mother in some spasm
Bears a base child and loathes it, so our best enthusiasm

Genders unlawful children, Anarchy
   Freedom's own Judas, the vile prodigal
Licence who steals the gold of Liberty
   And yet has nothing, Ignorance the real
One Fratricide since Cain, Envy the asp
That stings itself to anguish, Avarice whose palsied grasp

Is in its extent stiffened, monied Greed
   For whose dull appetite men waste away   320
Amid the whirr of wheels and are the seed
   Of things which slay their sower, these each day
Sees rife in England, and the gentle feet
Of Beauty tread no more the stones of each unlovely street.

What even Cromwell spared is desecrated
   By weed and worm, left to the stormy play
Of wind and beating snow, or renovated
   By more destructful hands: Time's worst decay
Will wreathe its ruins with some loveliness,
But these new Vandals can but make a rainproof barrenness.   330

Where is that Art which bade the Angels sing
   Through Lincoln's lofty choir, till the air
Seems from such marble harmonies to ring
   With sweeter song than common lips can dare
To draw from actual reed? ah! where is now
The cunning hand which made the flowering hawthorn branches
      bow

For Southwell's arch, and carved the House of One
   Who loved the lilies of the field with all
Our dearest English flowers? the same sun
   Rises for us: the seasons natural   340
Weave the same tapestry of green and grey:
The unchanged hills are with us: but that Spirit hath passed away.

And yet perchance it may be better so,
   For Tyranny is an incestuous Queen,
Murder her brother is her bedfellow,

And the Plague chambers with her: in obscene
And bloody paths her treacherous feet are set;
Better the empty desert and a soul inviolate!

For gentle brotherhood, the harmony
    Of living in the healthful air, the swift   350
Clean beauty of strong limbs when men are free
    And women chaste, these are the things which lift
Our souls up more than even Agnolo's
Gaunt blinded Sibyl poring o'er the scroll of human woes,

Or Titian's little maiden on the stair
    White as her own sweet lily, and as tall,
Or Mona Lisa smiling through her hair,—
    Ah! somehow life is bigger after all
Than any painted Angel could we see
The God that is within us! The old Greek serenity   360

Which curbs the passion of that level line
    Of marble youths, who with untroubled eyes
And chastened limbs ride round Athena's shrine
    And mirror her divine economies,
And balanced symmetry of what in man
Would else wage ceaseless warfare,—this at least within the span

Between our mother's kisses and the grave
    Might so inform our lives, that we could win
Such mighty empires that from her cave
    Temptation would grow hoarse, and pallid Sin   370
Would walk ashamed of his adulteries,
And Passion creep from out the House of Lust with startled eyes.

To make the Body and the Spirit one
    With all right things, till no thing live in vain
From morn to noon, but in sweet unison
    With every pulse of flesh and throb of brain
The Soul in flawless essence high enthroned,
Against all outer vain attack invincibly bastioned,

Mark with serene impartiality
   The strife of things, and yet be comforted,   380
Knowing that by the chain causality
   All separate existences are wed
Into one supreme whole, whose utterance
Is joy, or holier praise! ah! surely this were governance

Of Life in most august omnipresence,
   Through which the rational intellect would find
In passion its expression, and mere sense,
   Ignoble else, lend fire to the mind,
And being joined with it in harmony
More mystical than that which binds the stars planetary,   390

Strike from their several tones one octave chord
   Whose cadence being measureless would fly
Through all the circling spheres, then to its Lord
   Return refreshed with its new empery
And more exultant power,—this indeed
Could we but reach it were to find the last, the perfect creed.

Ah! it was easy when the world was young
   To keep one's life free and inviolate,
From our sad lips another song is rung,
   By our own hands our heads are desecrate,   400
Wanderers in drear exile, and dispossessed
Of what should be our own, we can but feed on wild unrest.

Somehow the grace, the bloom of things has flown,
   And of all men we are most wretched who
Must live each other's lives and not our own
   For very pity's sake and then undo
All that we lived for—it was otherwise
When soul and body seemed to blend in mystic symphonies.

But we have left those gentle haunts to pass
   With weary feet to the new Calvary,   410
Where we behold, as one who in a glass
   Sees his own face, self-slain Humanity,
And in the dumb reproach of that sad gaze
Learn what an awful phantom the red hand of man can raise.

O smitten mouth! O forehead crowned with thorn!
    O chalice of all common miseries!
Thou for our sakes that loved thee not hast borne
    An agony of endless centuries,
And we were vain and ignorant nor knew   419
That when we stabbed thy heart it was our own real hearts we slew.

Being ourselves the sowers and the seeds,
    The night that covers and the lights that fade,
The spear that pierces and the side that bleeds,
    The lips betraying and the life betrayed;
The deep hath calm: the moon hath rest: but we
Lords of the natural world are yet our own dread enemy.

Is this the end of all that primal force
    Which, in its changes being still the same,
From eyeless Chaos cleft its upward course,
    Through ravenous seas and whirling rocks and flame,   430
Till the suns met in heaven and began
Their cycles, and the morning stars sang, and the Word was Man!

Nay, nay, we are but crucified, and though
    The bloody sweat falls from our brows like rain,
Loosen the nails—we shall come down I know,
    Staunch the red wounds—we shall be whole again,
No need have we of hyssop-laden rod,
That which is purely human, that is Godlike, that is God.

Athanasia

To that gaunt House of Art which lacks for naught
    Of all the great things men have saved from Time,
The withered body of a girl was brought,
    Dead ere the world's glad youth had touched its prime,
And seen by lonely Arabs lying hid
In the dim womb of some black pyramid.

But when they had unloosed the linen band
   Which swathed the Egyptian's body,—lo! was found
Closed in the wasted hollow of her hand
   A little seed, which sown in English ground   10
Did wondrous snow of starry blossoms bear,
And spread rich odours through our springtide air.

With such strange arts this flower did allure
   That all forgotten was the asphodel,
And the brown bee, the lily's paramour,
   Forsook the cup where he was wont to dwell,
For not a thing of earth it seemed to be,
But stolen from some heavenly Arcady.

In vain the sad narcissus, wan and white
   At its own beauty, hung across the stream,   20
The purple dragon-fly had no delight
   With its gold dust to make his wings a-gleam,
Ah! no delight the jasmine-bloom to kiss,
Or brush the rain-pearls from the eucharis.

For love of it the passionate nightingale
   Forgot the hills of Thrace, the cruel king,
And the pale dove no longer cared to sail
   Through the wet woods at time of blossoming,
But round this flower of Egypt sought to float,
With silvered wing and amethystine throat.   30

While the hot sun blazed in his tower of blue
   A cooling wind crept from the land of snows,
And the warm south with tender tears of dew
   Drenched its white leaves when Hesperos uprose
Amid those sea-green meadows of the sky
On which the scarlet bars of sunset lie.

But when o'er wastes of lily-haunted field
   The tired birds had stayed their amorous tune,
And broad and glittering like an argent shield
   High in the sapphire heavens hung the moon,   40
Did no strange dream or evil memory make
Each tremulous petal of its blossoms shake?

Ah no! to this bright flower a thousand years
   Seemed but the lingering of a summer's day,
It never knew the tide of cankering fears
   Which turn a boy's gold hair to withered grey,
The dread desire of death it never knew,
Or how all folk that they were born must rue.

For we to death with pipe and dancing go,
   Nor would we pass the ivory gate again,   50
As some sad river wearied of its flow
   Through the dull plains, the haunts of common men,
Leaps lover-like into the terrible sea!
And counts it gain to die so gloriously.

We mar our lordly strength in barren strife
   With the world's legions led by clamorous care,
It never feels decay but gathers life
   From the pure sunlight and the supreme air,
We live beneath Time's wasting sovereignty,
It is the child of all eternity.   60

The New Helen

Where hast thou been since round the walls of Troy
   The sons of God fought in that great emprise?
      Why dost thou walk our common earth again?
Hast thou forgotten that impassioned boy,
   His purple galley, and his Tyrian men,
   And treacherous Aphrodite's mocking eyes?
For surely it was thou, who, like a star
   Hung in the silver silence of the night,
   Didst lure the Old World's chivalry and might
Into the clamorous crimson waves of war!   10

Or didst thou rule the fire-laden moon?
   In amorous Sidon was thy temple built
      Over the light and laughter of the sea?
   Where, behind lattice scarlet-wrought and gilt,
      Some brown-limbed girl did weave thee tapestry,

All through the waste and wearied hours of noon;
Till her wan cheek with flame of passion burned,
   And she rose up the sea-washed lips to kiss
Of some glad Cyprian sailor, safe returned
   From Calpé and the cliffs of Herakles!   20

No! thou art Helen, and none other one!
   It was for thee that young Sarpedôn died,
      And Memnôn's manhood was untimely spent;
   It was for thee gold-crested Hector tried
With Thetis' child that evil race to run,
      In the last year of thy beleaguerment;
Ay! even now the glory of thy fame
   Burns in those fields of trampled asphodel,
   Where the high lords whom Ilion knew so well
Clash ghostly shields, and call upon thy name.   30

Where hast thou been? in that enchanted land
   Whose slumbering vales forlorn Calypso knew,
      Where never mower rose at break of day
   But all unswathed the trammelling grasses grew,
And the sad shepherd saw the tall corn stand
      Till summer's red had changed to withered gray?
Didst thou lie there by some Lethæan stream
   Deep brooding on thine ancient memory,
   The crash of broken spears, the fiery gleam
      From shivered helm, the Grecian battle-cry?   40

Nay, thou wert hidden in that hollow hill
   With one who is forgotten utterly,
      That discrowned Queen men call the Erycine;
   Hidden away that never mightst thou see
      The face of Her, before whose mouldering shrine
To-day at Rome the silent nations kneel;
   Who gat from Love no joyous gladdening,
      But only Love's intolerable pain,
      Only a sword to pierce her heart in twain,
Only the bitterness of child-bearing.   50

The lotos-leaves which heal the wounds of Death
   Lie in thy hand; O, be thou kind to me,
      While yet I know the summer of my days;
For hardly can my tremulous lips draw breath
      To fill the silver trumpet with thy praise,
   So bowed am I before thy mystery;
So bowed and broken on Love's terrible wheel,
   That I have lost all hope and heart to sing,
   Yet care I not what ruin time may bring
If in thy temple thou wilt let me kneel.   60

Alas, alas, thou wilt not tarry here,
   But, like that bird, the servant of the sun,
      Who flies before the northwind and the night,
So wilt thou fly our evil land and drear,
      Back to the tower of thine old delight,
   And the red lips of young Euphorion;
Nor shall I ever see thy face again,
   But in this poisonous garden-close must stay,
Crowning my brows with the thorn-crown of pain,
   Till all my loveless life shall pass away.   70

O Helen! Helen! Helen! yet a while,
   Yet for a little while, O, tarry here,
      Till the dawn cometh and the shadows flee!
For in the gladsome sunlight of thy smile
      Of heaven or hell I have no thought or fear,
   Seeing I know no other god but thee:
No other god save him, before whose feet
   In nets of gold the tired planets move,
   The incarnate spirit of spiritual love
Who in thy body holds his joyous seat.   80

Thou wert not born as common women are!
   But, girt with silver splendour of the foam,
      Didst from the depths of sapphire seas arise!
And at thy coming some immortal star,
      Bearded with flame, blazed in the Eastern skies,
   And waked the shepherds on thine island-home.
Thou shalt not die: no asps of Egypt creep

Close at thy heels to taint the delicate air;
   No sullen-blooming poppies stain thy hair,
Those scarlet heralds of eternal sleep.   90

Lily of love, pure and inviolate!
   Tower of ivory! red rose of fire!
      Thou hast come down our darkness to illume:
For we, close-caught in the wide nets of Fate,
      Wearied with waiting for the World's Desire,
         Aimlessly wandered in the House of gloom,
Aimlessly sought some slumberous anodyne
      For wasted lives, for lingering wretchedness,
Till we beheld thy re-arisen shrine,
   And the white glory of thy loveliness.   100

Panthea

Nay, let us walk from fire unto fire,
   From passionate pain to deadlier delight,—
I am too young to live without desire,
   Too young art thou to waste this summer night
Asking those idle questions which of old
Man sought of seer and oracle, and no reply was told.

For, sweet, to feel is better than to know,
   And wisdom is a childless heritage,
One pulse of passion—youth's first fiery glow,—
   Are worth the hoarded proverbs of the sage: 10
Vex not thy soul with dead philosophy,
Have we not lips to kiss with, hearts to love, and eyes to see!

Dost thou not hear the murmuring nightingale
   Like water bubbling from a silver jar,
So soft she sings the envious moon is pale,
   That high in heaven she is hung so far
She cannot hear that love-enraptured tune,—
Mark how she wreathes each horn with mist, yon late and labour-
   ing moon.

White lilies, in whose cups the gold bees dream,
   The fallen snow of petals where the breeze   20
Scatters the chestnut blossom, or the gleam
   Of boyish limbs in water,—are not these
Enough for thee, dost thou desire more?
Alas! the Gods will give nought else from their eternal store.

For our high Gods have sick and wearied grown
   Of all our endless sins, our vain endeavour
For wasted days of youth to make atone
   By pain or prayer or priest, and never, never,
Hearken they now to either good or ill,
But send their rain upon the just and the unjust at will.   30

They sit at ease, our Gods they sit at ease,
   Strewing with leaves of rose their scented wine,
They sleep, they sleep, beneath the rocking trees
   Where asphodel and yellow lotus twine,
Mourning the old glad days before they knew
What evil things the heart of man could dream, and dreaming do.

And far beneath the brazen floor they see
   Like swarming flies the crowd of little men,
The bustle of small lives, then wearily
   Back to their lotus-haunts they turn again   40
Kissing each other's mouths, and mix more deep
The poppy-seeded draught which brings soft purple-lidded sleep.

There all day long the golden-vestured sun,
   Their torch-bearer, stands with his torch a-blaze,
And, when the gaudy web of noon is spun
   By its twelve maidens, through the crimson haze
Fresh from Endymion's arms comes forth the moon,
And the immortal Gods in toils of mortal passions swoon.

There walks Queen Juno through some dewy mead
   Her grand white feet flecked with the saffron dust   50
Of wind-stirred lilies, while young Ganymede
   Leaps in the hot and amber-foaming must,
His curls all tossed, as when the eagle bare
The frightened boy from Ida through the blue Ionian air.

There in the green heart of some garden close
  Queen Venus with the shepherd at her side,
Her warm soft body like the briar rose
  Which would be white yet blushes at its pride,
Laughs low for love, till jealous Salmacis   59
Peers through the myrtle-leaves and sighs for pain of lonely bliss.

There never does that dreary north-wind blow
  Which leaves our English forests bleak and bare,
Nor ever falls the swift white-feathered snow,
  Nor ever doth the red-toothed lightning dare
To wake them in the silver-fretted night
When we lie weeping for some sweet sad sin, some dead delight.

Alas! they know the far Lethæan spring,
  The violet-hidden waters well they know,
Where one whose feet with tired wandering
  Are faint and broken may take heart and go,   70
And from those dark depths cool and crystalline
Drink, and draw balm, and sleep for sleepless souls, and anodyne.

But we oppress our natures, God or Fate
  Is our enemy, we starve and feed
On vain repentance—O we are born too late!
  What balm for us in bruisèd poppy seed
Who crowd into one finite pulse of time
The joy of infinite love and the fierce pain of infinite crime!

O we are wearied of this sense of guilt,
  Wearied of pleasure's paramour despair,   80
Wearied of every temple we have built,
  Wearied of every right, unanswered, prayer,
For man is weak; God sleeps: and heaven is high:
One fiery-coloured moment: one great love; and lo! we die.

Ah! but no ferry-man with labouring pole
  Nears his black shallop to the flowerless strand,
No little coin of bronze can bring the soul

Over Death's river to the sunless land,
Victim and wine and vow are all in vain,   89
The tomb is sealed; the soldiers watch; the dead rise not again.

We are resolved into the supreme air,
    We are made one with what we touch and see,
With our heart's blood each crimson sun is fair,
    With our young lives each spring-impassioned tree
Flames into green, the wildest beasts that range
The moor our kinsmen are, all life is one, and all is change.

With beat of systole and of diastole
    One grand great life throbs through earth's giant heart,
And mighty waves of single Being roll
    From nerve-less germ to man, for we are part   100
Of every rock and bird and beast and hill,
One with the things that prey on us, and one with what we kill.

From lower cells of waking life we pass
    To full perfection; thus the world grows old:
We who are godlike now were once a mass
    Of quivering purple flecked with bars of gold,
Unsentient or of joy or misery,
And tossed in terrible tangles of some wild and wind-swept sea.

This hot hard flame with which our bodies burn
    Will make some meadow blaze with daffodil,   110
Ay! and those argent breasts of thine will turn
    To water-lilies; the brown fields men till
Will be more fruitful for our love to-night,
Nothing is lost in nature, all things live in Death's despite.

The boy's first kiss, the hyacinth's first bell,
    The man's last passion, and the last red spear
That from the lily leaps, the asphodel
    Which will not let its blossoms blow for fear
Of too much beauty, and the timid shame   119
Of the young bride-groom at his lover's eyes,—these with the same

One sacrament are consecrate, the earth
   Not we alone hath passions hymeneal,
The yellow buttercups that shake for mirth
   At daybreak know a pleasure not less real
Than we do when in some fresh-blossoming wood
We draw the spring into our hearts and feel that life is good.

So when men bury us beneath the yew
   Thy crimson-stainèd mouth a rose will be,
And thy soft eyes lush bluebells dimmed with dew,
   And when the white narcissus wantonly   130
Kisses the wind its playmate some faint joy
Will thrill our dust, and we will be again fond maid and boy.

And thus without life's conscious torturing pain
   In some sweet flower we will feel the sun,
And from the linnet's throat will sing again,
   And as two gorgeous-mailèd snakes will run
Over our graves, or as two tigers creep
Through the hot jungle where the yellow-eyed huge lions sleep

And give them battle! How my heart leaps up
   To think of that grand living after death   140
In beast and bird and flower, when this cup,
   Being filled too full of spirit, bursts for breath,
And with the pale leaves of some autumn day
The soul earth's earliest conqueror becomes earth's last great prey.

O think of it! We shall inform ourselves
   Into all sensuous life, the goat-foot Faun,
The Centaur, or the merry bright-eyed Elves
   That leave their dancing rings to spite the dawn
Upon the meadows, shall not be more near
Than you and I to nature's mysteries, for we shall hear   150

The thrush's heart beat, and the daisies grow,
   And the wan snowdrop sighing for the sun
On sunless days in winter, we shall know
   By whom the silver gossamer is spun,
Who paints the diapered fritillaries,
On what wide wings from shivering pine to pine the eagle flies.

Ay! had we never loved at all, who knows
   If yonder daffodil had lured the bee
Into its gilded womb, or any rose
   Had hung with crimson lamps its little tree!   160
Methinks no leaf would ever bud in spring,
But for the lovers' lips that kiss, the poets' lips that sing.

Is the light vanished from our golden sun,
   Or is this dædal-fashioned earth less fair,
That we are nature's heritors, and one
   With every pulse of life that beats the air?
Rather new suns across the sky shall pass,
New splendour come unto the flower, new glory to the grass.

And we two lovers shall not sit afar,
   Critics of nature, but the joyous sea   170
Shall be our raiment, and the bearded star
   Shoot arrows at our pleasure! We shall be
Part of the mighty universal whole,
And through all æons mix and mingle with the Kosmic Soul!

We shall be notes in that great Symphony
   Whose cadence circles through the rhythmic spheres,
And all the live World's throbbing heart shall be
   One with our heart, the stealthy creeping years
Have lost their terrors now, we shall not die,
The Universe itself shall be our Immortality!   180

Phèdre

How vain and dull this common world must seem
   To such a One as thou, who should'st have talked
   At Florence with Mirandola, or walked
Through the cool olives of the Academe:
Thou should'st have gathered reeds from a green stream
   For Goat-foot Pan's shrill piping, and have played
   With the white girls in that Phæacian glade
Where grave Odysseus wakened from his dream.

Ah! surely once some urn of Attic clay
   Held thy wan dust, and thou hast come again   10
   Back to this common world so dull and vain,
For thou wert weary of the sunless day,
   The heavy fields of scentless asphodel,
   The loveless lips with which men kiss in Hell.

Queen Henrietta Maria

In the lone tent, waiting for victory,
   She stands with eyes marred by the mists of pain,
   Like some wan lily overdrenched with rain:
The clamorous clang of arms, the ensanguined sky,
War's ruin, and the wreck of chivalry,
   To her proud soul no common fear can bring:
   Bravely she tarrieth for her Lord the King,
Her soul a-flame with passionate ecstasy.
O Hair of Gold! O Crimson Lips! O Face
   Made for the luring and the love of man!   10
   With thee I do forget the toil and stress,
The loveless road that knows no resting place,
   Time's straitened pulse, the soul's dread weariness,
   My freedom, and my life republican!

Louis Napoleon

Eagle of Austerlitz! where were thy wings
     When far away upon a barbarous strand,
     In fight unequal, by an obscure hand,
Fell the last scion of thy brood of Kings!

Poor boy! thou shalt not flaunt thy cloak of red,
     Or ride in state through Paris in the van
     Of thy returning legions, but instead
Thy mother France, free and republican,

Shall on thy dead and crownless forehead place
    The better laurels of a soldier's crown,   10
    That not dishonoured should thy soul go down
To tell the mighty Sire of thy race

That France hath kissed the mouth of Liberty,
    And found it sweeter than his honied bees,
    And that the giant wave Democracy
Breaks on the shores where Kings lay couched at ease.

Madonna Mia

A lily-girl, not made for this world's pain,
    With brown, soft hair close braided by her ears,
    And longing eyes half veiled by slumberous tears
Like bluest water seen through mists of rain:
Pale cheeks whereon no love hath left its stain,
    Red underlip drawn in for fear of love,
    And white throat, whiter than the silvered dove,
Through whose wan marble creeps one purple vein.
Yet, though my lips shall praise her without cease,
    Even to kiss her feet I am not bold,   10
    Being o'ershadowed by the wings of awe.
Like Dante, when he stood with Beatrice
    Beneath the flaming Lion's breast, and saw
    The seventh Crystal, and the Stair of Gold.

Roses and Rue

I

I remember we used to meet
    By a garden seat,
And you warbled each pretty word
    With the air of a bird,

And your voice had a quaver in it
   Just like a linnet,
And shook with the last full note
   As the thrush's throat.

And your eyes, they were green and grey,
   Like an April day,   10
But lit into amethyst
   When I stooped and kissed.

And your hair—well, I never could tie it,
   For it ran all riot
Like a tangled sunbeam of gold,
   Great fold upon fold.

II

You were always afraid of a shower,
   (Just like a flower!);
I remember you started and ran
   When the rain began.   20

I remember I never could catch you,
   For no one could match you;
You had wonderful luminous fleet
   Little wings to your feet.

Yet you somehow would give me the prize,
   With a laugh in your eyes,
The rose from your breast, or the bliss
   Of a single swift kiss

On your neck with its marble hue,
   And its vein of blue—   30
How these passionate memories bite
   In my heart as I write!

III

I remember so well the room,
  And the lilac bloom
That beat at the dripping pane,
  In the warm June rain.

And the colour of your gown,
  It was amber-brown,
And two little satin bows
  From your shoulders rose.   40

And the handkerchief of French lace
  Which you held to your face—
Had a tear-drop left a stain?
  Or was it the rain?

'You have only wasted your life'—
  (Ah! there was the knife!)
Those were the words you said,
  As you turned your head.

I had wasted my boyhood, true,
  But it was for you,   50
You had poets enough on the shelf,
  I gave you myself!

IV

Well, if my heart must break,
  Dear Love, for your sake,
It will break in music, I know;
  Poets' hearts break so.
But strange that I was not told
  That the brain can hold
In a tiny ivory cell
  God's Heaven and Hell.   60

Portia

I marvel not Bassanio was so bold
   To peril all he had upon the lead,
   Or that proud Aragon bent low his head,
Or that Morocco's fiery heart grew cold:
For in that gorgeous dress of beaten gold
   Which is more golden than the golden sun,
   No woman Veronesé looked upon
Was half so fair as Thou whom I behold.
Yet fairer when with wisdom as your shield
   The sober-suited lawyer's gown you donned   10
And would not let the laws of Venice yield
   Antonio's heart to that accursèd Jew—
   O Portia! take my heart: it is thy due:
I think I will not quarrel with the Bond.

Apologia

Is it thy will that I should wax and wane,
   Barter my cloth of gold for hodden grey,
And at thy pleasure weave that web of pain
   Whose brightest threads are each a wasted day?

Is it thy will—Love that I love so well—
   That my Soul's House should be a tortured spot
Wherein, like evil paramours, must dwell
   The quenchless flame, the worm that dieth not?

Nay, if it be thy will I shall endure,
   And sell ambition at the common mart,   10
And let dull failure be my vestiture,
   And sorrow dig its grave within my heart.

Perchance it may be better so—at least
   I have not made my heart a heart of stone,
Nor starved my boyhood of its goodly feast,
   Nor walked where Beauty is a thing unknown.

Many a man hath done so; sought to fence
  In straitened bonds the soul that should be free,
Trodden the dusty road of common sense,
  While all the forest sang of liberty,   20

Not marking how the spotted hawk in flight
  Passed on wide pinion through the lofty air,
To where some steep untrodden moutain height
  Caught the last tresses of the Sun God's hair.

Or how the little flower he trod upon,
  The daisy, that white-feathered shield of gold,
Followed with wistful eyes the wandering sun
  Content if once its leaves were aureoled.

But surely it is something to have been
  The best belovèd for a little while,   30
To have walked hand in hand with Love, and seen
  His purple wings flit once across thy smile.

Ay! though the gorgèd asp of passion feed
  On my boy's heart, yet have I burst the bars,
Stood face to face with Beauty, known indeed
  The Love which moves the Sun and all the stars!

Quia Multum Amavi

Dear Heart I think the young impassioned priest
  When first he takes from out the hidden shrine
His God imprisoned in the Eucharist,
  And eats the bread, and drinks the dreadful wine,

Feels not such awful wonder as I felt
  When first my smitten eyes beat full on thee,
And all night long before thy feet I knelt
  Till thou wert wearied of Idolatry.

Ah! had'st thou liked me less and loved me more,
   Through all those summer days of joy and rain,   10
I had not now been sorrow's heritor,
   Or stood a lackey in the House of Pain.

Yet, though remorse, youth's white-faced seneschal,
   Tread on my heels with all his retinue,
I am most glad I loved thee—think of all
   The suns that go to make one speedwell blue!

Silentium Amoris

As oftentimes the too resplendent sun
   Hurries the pallid and reluctant moon
Back to her sombre cave, ere she hath won
   A single ballad from the nightingale,
   So doth thy Beauty make my lips to fail,
And all my sweetest singing out of tune.

And as at dawn across the level mead
   On wings impetuous some wind will come,
And with its too harsh kisses break the reed
   Which was its only instrument of song,   10
   So my too stormy passions work me wrong,
And for excess of Love my Love is dumb.

But surely unto Thee mine eyes did show
   Why I am silent, and my lute unstrung;
Else it were better we should part, and go,
   Thou to some lips of sweeter melody,
   And I to nurse the barren memory
Of unkissed kisses, and songs never sung.

Her Voice

The wild bee reels from bough to bough
　With his furry coat and his gauzy wing,
Now in a lily-cup, and now
　　Setting a jacinth bell a-swing,
　　　In his wandering;
Sit closer love: it was here I trow
　　I made that vow,

Swore that two lives should be like one
　As long as the sea-gull loved the sea,
As long as the sunflower sought the sun,—　　10
　　It shall be, I said, for eternity
　　　'Twixt you and me!
Dear friend, those times are over and done,
　　Love's web is spun.

Look upward where the poplar trees
　Sway and sway in the summer air,
Here in the valley never a breeze
　　Scatters the thistledown, but there
　　　Great winds blow fair
From the mighty murmuring mystical seas,　　20
　　And the wave-lashed leas.

Look upward where the white gull screams,
　What does it see that we do not see?
Is that a star? or the lamp that gleams
　　On some outward voyaging argosy,—
　　　Ah! can it be
We have lived our lives in a land of dreams!
　　How sad it seems.

Sweet, there is nothing left to say
　But this, that love is never lost,　　30
Keen winter stabs the breasts of May
　　Whose crimson roses burst his frost,

Ships tempest-tossed
Will find a harbour in some bay,
    And so we may.

And there is nothing left to do
    But to kiss once again, and part,
Nay, there is nothing we should rue,
    I have my beauty,—you your Art,
        Nay, do not start,   40
One world was not enough for two
    Like me and you.

My Voice

Within this restless, hurried, modern world
    We took our hearts' full pleasure—You and I,
And now the white sails of our ship are furled,
    And spent the lading of our argosy.

Wherefore my cheeks before their time are wan,
    For very weeping is my gladness fled,
Sorrow has paled my young mouth's vermilion,
    And Ruin draws the curtains of my bed.

But all this crowded life has been to thee
    No more than lyre, or lute, or subtle spell   10
Of viols, or the music of the sea
    That sleeps, a mimic echo, in the shell.

Γλυκύπικρος Ἔρως[1]

Sweet I blame you not for mine the fault was, had I not been made
    of common clay
I had climbed the higher heights unclimbed yet, seen the fuller air,
    the larger day.

[1] Bittersweet Love.

From the wildness of my wasted passion I had struck a better,
clearer song,
Lit some lighter light of freer freedom, battled with some Hydra-
headed wrong.

Had my lips been smitten into music by the kisses that but made
them bleed,
You had walked with Bice and the angels on that verdant and
enamelled mead.

I had trod the road which Dante treading saw the suns of seven
circles shine,
Ay! perchance had seen the heavens opening, as they opened to the
Florentine.

And the mighty nations would have crowned me, who am crown-
less now and without name,
And some orient dawn had found me kneeling on the threshold of
the House of Fame. 10

I had sat within that marble circle where the oldest bard is as the
young,
And the pipe is ever dropping honey, and the lyre's strings are ever
strung.

Keats had lifted up his hymenæal curls from out the poppy-seeded
wine,
With ambrosial mouth had kissed my forehead, clasped the hand of
noble love in mine.

And at springtide, when the apple-blossoms brush the burnished
bosom of the dove,
Two young lovers lying in an orchard would have read the story of
our love.

Would have read the legend of my passion, known the bitter secret
of my heart,
Kissed as we have kissed, but never parted as we two are fated now
to part.

For the crimson flower of our life is eaten by the cankerworm of
    truth,
And no hand can gather up the fallen withered petals of the rose of
    youth.   20

Yet I am not sorry that I loved you—ah! what else had I a boy to
    do,—
For the hungry teeth of time devour, and the silent-footed years
    pursue.

Rudderless, we drift athwart a tempest, and when once the storm
    of youth is past,
Without lyre, without lute or chorus, Death the silent pilot comes
    at last.

And within the grave there is no pleasure, for the blind-worm
    battens on the root,
And Desire shudders into ashes, and the tree of Passion bears no
    fruit.

Ah! what else had I to do but love you, God's own mother was less
    dear to me,
And less dear the Cytheræan rising like an argent lily from the sea.

I have made my choice, have lived my poems, and, though youth is
    gone in wasted days,
I have found the lover's crown of myrtle better than the poet's
    crown of bays.   30

The Garden of Eros

It is full summer now, the heart of June,
    Not yet the sun-burnt reapers are a-stir
Upon the upland meadow where too soon
    Rich autumn time, the season's usurer,
Will lend his hoarded gold to all the trees,
And see his treasure scattered by the wild and spend-thrift breeze.

Too soon indeed! yet here the daffodil,
    That love-child of the Spring, has lingered on
To vex the rose with jealousy, and still
    The harebell spreads her azure pavilion,   10
And like a strayed and wandering reveller
Abandoned of its brothers, whom long since June's messenger

The missel-thrush has frighted from the glade,
    One pale narcissus loiters fearfully
Close to a shadowy nook, where half afraid
    Of their own loveliness some violets lie
That will not look the gold sun in the face
For fear of too much splendour,—ah! methinks it is a place

Which should be trodden by Persephone
    When wearied of the flowerless fields of Dis!   20
Or danced on by the lads of Arcady!
    The hidden secret of eternal bliss
Known to the Grecian here a man might find,
Ah! you and I may find it now if Love and Sleep be kind.

There are the flowers which mourning Herakles
    Strewed on the tomb of Hylas, columbine,
Its white doves all a-flutter where the breeze
    Kissed them too harshly, the small celandine,
That yellow-kirtled chorister of eve,   29
And lilac lady's-smock,—but let them bloom alone, and leave

Yon spired holly-hock red-crocketed
    To sway its silent chimes, else must the bee,
Its little bellringer, go seek instead
    Some other pleasaunce; the anemone
That weeps at daybreak, like a silly girl
Before her love, and hardly lets the butterflies unfurl

Their painted wings beside it,—bid it pine
    In pale virginity; the winter snow
Will suit it better than those lips of thine

Whose fires would but scorch it, rather go   40
And pluck that amorous flower which blooms alone,
Fed by the pander wind with dust of kisses not its own.

The trumpet-mouths of red convolvulus
    So dear to maidens, creamy meadow-sweet
Whiter than Juno's throat and odorous
    As all Arabia, hyacinths the feet
Of Huntress Dian would be loth to mar
For any dappled fawn,—pluck these, and those fond flowers which
    are

Fairer than what Queen Venus trod upon
    Beneath the pines of Ida, eucharis,   50
That morning star which does not dread the sun,
    And budding marjoram which but to kiss
Would sweeten Cytheræa's lips and make
Adonis jealous,—these for thy head,—and for thy girdle take

Yon curving spray of purple clematis
    Whose gorgeous dye outflames the Tyrian King,
And fox-gloves with their nodding chalices,
    But that one narciss which the startled Spring
Let from her kirtle fall when first she heard
In her own woods the wild tempestuous song of summer's
    bird,   60

Ah! leave it for a subtle memory
    Of those sweet tremulous days of rain and sun,
When April laughed between her tears to see
    The early primrose with shy footsteps run
From the gnarled oak-tree roots till all the wold,
Spite of its brown and trampled leaves, grew bright with shimmer-
    ing gold.

Nay, pluck it too, it is not half so sweet
    As thou thyself, my soul's idolatry!
And when thou art a-wearied at thy feet

Shall oxlips weave their brightest tapestry, 70
For thee the woodbine shall forget its pride
And vail its tangled whorls, and thou shalt walk on daisies pied.

And I will cut a reed by yonder spring
   And make the wood-gods jealous, and old Pan
Wonder what young intruder dares to sing
   In these still haunts, where never foot of man
Should tread at evening, lest he chance to spy
The marble limbs of Artemis and all her company.

And I will tell thee why the jacinth wears
   Such dread embroidery of dolorous moan, 80
And why the hapless nightingale forbears
   To sing her song at noon, but weeps alone
When the fleet swallow sleeps, and rich men feast,
And why the laurel trembles when she sees the lightening east.

And I will sing how sad Proserpina
   Unto a grave and gloomy Lord was wed,
And lure the silver-breasted Helena
   Back from the lotus meadows of the dead,
So shalt thou see that awful loveliness
For which two mighty Hosts met fearfully in war's abyss! 90

And then I'll pipe to thee that Grecian tale
   How Cynthia loves the lad Endymion,
And hidden in a grey and misty veil
   Hies to the cliffs of Latmos once the Sun
Leaps from his ocean bed in fruitless chase
Of those pale flying feet which fade away in his embrace.

And if my flute can breathe sweet melody,
   We may behold Her face who long ago
Dwelt among men by the Ægean sea,
   And whose sad house with pillaged portico 100
And friezeless wall and columns toppled down
Looms o'er the ruins of that fair and violet-cinctured town.

Spirit of Beauty! tarry still a-while,
  They are not dead, thine ancient votaries,
Some few there are to whom thy radiant smile
  Is better than a thousand victories,
Though all the nobly slain of Waterloo
Rise up in wrath against them! tarry still, there are a few

Who for thy sake would give their manlihood
  And consecrate their being, I at least   110
Have done so, made thy lips my daily food,
  And in thy temples found a goodlier feast
Than this starved age can give me, spite of all
Its new-found creeds so sceptical and so dogmatical.

Here not Cephissos, not Ilissos flows,
  The woods of white Colonos are not here,
On our bleak hills the olive never blows,
  No simple priest conducts his lowing steer
Up the steep marble way, nor through the town
Do laughing maidens bear to thee the crocus-flowered gown. 120

Yet tarry! for the boy who loved thee best,
  Whose very name should be a memory
To make thee linger, sleeps in silent rest
  Beneath the Roman walls, and melody
Still mourns her sweetest lyre, none can play
The lute of Adonais, with his lips Song passed away.

Nay, when Keats died the Muses still had left
  One silver voice to sing his threnody,
But ah! too soon of it we were bereft
  When on that riven night and stormy sea   130
Panthea claimed her singer as her own,
And slew the mouth that praised her; since which time we walk
    alone,

Save for that fiery heart, that morning star
  Of re-arisen England, whose clear eye
Saw from our tottering throne and waste of war
  The grand Greek limbs of young Democracy

Rise mightily like Hesperus and bring
The great Republic! him at least thy love hath taught to sing,

And he hath been with thee at Thessaly,
   And seen white Atalanta fleet of foot   140
In passionless and fierce virginity
   Hunting the tuskéd boar, his honied lute
Hath pierced the cavern of the hollow hill,
And Venus laughs to know one knee will bow before her still.

And he hath kissed the lips of Proserpine,
   And sung the Galilæan's requiem,
That wounded forehead dashed with blood and wine
   He hath discrowned, the Ancient Gods in him
Have found their last, most ardent worshipper,
And the new Sign grows grey and dim before its conqueror.   150

Spirit of Beauty! tarry with us still,
   It is not quenched the torch of poesy,
The star that shook above the Eastern hill
   Holds unassailed its argent armoury
From all the gathering gloom and fretful fight—
O tarry with us still! for through the long and common night,

Morris, our sweet and simple Chaucer's child,
   Dear heritor of Spenser's tuneful reed,
With soft and sylvan pipe has oft beguiled
   The weary soul of man in troublous need,   160
And from the far and flowerless fields of ice
Has brought fair flowers meet to make an earthly paradise.

We know them all, Gudrun the strong men's bride,
   Aslaug and Olafson we know them all,
How giant Grettir fought and Sigurd died,
   And what enchantment held the king in thrall
When lonely Brynhild wrestled with the powers
That war against all passion, ah! how oft through summer hours,

Long listless summer hours when the noon
   Being enamoured of a damask rose   170
Forgets to journey westward, till the moon
   The pale usurper of its tribute grows
From a thin sickle to a silver shield
And chides its loitering car—how oft, in some cool grassy field

Far from the cricket-ground and noisy eight,
   At Bagley, where the rustling bluebells come
Almost before the blackbird finds a mate
   And overstay the swallow, and the hum
Of many murmuring bees flits through the leaves,
Have I lain poring on the dreamy tales his fancy weaves,   180

And through their unreal woes and mimic pain
   Wept for myself, and so was purified,
And in their simple mirth grew glad again;
   For as I sailed upon that pictured tide
The strength and splendour of the storm was mine
Without the storm's red ruin, for the singer is divine,

The little laugh of water falling down
   Is not so musical, the clammy gold
Close hoarded in the tiny waxen town
   Has less of sweetness in it, and the old   190
Half-withered reeds that waved in Arcady
Touched by his lips break forth again to fresher harmony.

Spirit of Beauty tarry yet a-while!
   Although the cheating merchants of the mart
With iron roads profane our lovely isle,
   And break on whirling wheels the limbs of Art,
Ay! though the crowded factories beget
The blind-worm Ignorance that slays the soul, O tarry yet!

For One at least there is,—He bears his name
   From Dante and the seraph Gabriel,—   200
Whose double laurels burn with deathless flame

To light thine altar; He too loves thee well,
Who saw old Merlin lured in Vivien's snare,
And the white feet of angels coming down the golden stair,

Loves thee so well, that all the World for him
    A gorgeous-coloured vestiture must wear,
And Sorrow take a purple diadem,
    Or else be no more Sorrow, and Despair
Gild its own thorns, and Pain, like Adon, be
Even in anguish beautiful;—such is the empery   210

Which Painters hold, and such the heritage
    This gentle solemn Spirit doth possess,
Being a better mirror of his age
    In all his pity, love, and weariness,
Than those who can but copy common things,
And leave the Soul unpainted with its mighty questionings.

But they are few, and all romance has flown,
    And men can prophesy about the sun,
And lecture on his arrows—how, alone,
    Through a waste void the soulless atoms run,   220
How from each tree its weeping nymph has fled,
And that no more 'mid English reeds a Naïad shows her head.

Methinks these new Actæons boast too soon
    That they have spied on beauty; what if we
Have analyzed the rainbow, robbed the moon
    Of her most ancient, chastest mystery,
Shall I, the last Endymion, lose all hope
Because rude eyes peer at my mistress through a telescope!

What profit if this scientific age
    Burst through our gates with all its retinue   230
Of modern miracles! Can it assuage
    One lover's breaking heart? what can it do
To make one life more beautiful, one day
More god-like in its period? but now the Age of Clay

Returns in horrid cycle, and the earth
  Hath borne again a noisy progeny
Of ignorant Titans, whose ungodly birth
  Hurls them against the august hierarchy
Which sat upon Olympus, to the Dust
They have appealed, and to that barren arbiter they must   240

Repair for judgment, let them, if they can,
  From Natural Warfare and insensate Chance,
Create the new Ideal rule for man!
  Methinks that was not my inheritance;
For I was nurtured otherwise, my soul
Passes from higher heights of life to a more supreme goal.

Lo! while we spake the earth did turn away
  Her visage from the God, and Hecate's boat
Rose silver-laden, till the jealous day
  Blew all its torches out: I did not note   250
The waning hours, to young Endymions
Time's palsied fingers count in vain his rosary of suns!

Mark how the yellow iris wearily
  Leans back its throat, as though it would be kissed
By its false chamberer, the dragon-fly,
  Who, like a blue vein on a girl's white wrist,
Sleeps on that snowy primrose of the night,
Which 'gins to flush with crimson shame, and die beneath the
      light.

Come let us go, against the pallid shield
  Of the wan sky the almond blossoms gleam,   260
The corn-crake nested in the unmown field
  Answers its mate, across the misty stream
On fitful wing the startled curlews fly,
And in his sedgy bed the lark, for joy that Day is nigh,

Scatters the pearlèd dew from off the grass,
  In tremulous ecstasy to greet the sun,
Who soon in gilded panoply will pass

Forth from yon orange-curtained pavilion
Hung in the burning east, see, the red rim
O'ertops the expectant hills! it is the God! for love of him   270

Already the shrill lark is out of sight,
    Flooding with waves of song this silent dell,—
Ah! there is something more in that bird's flight
    Than could be tested in a crucible!—
But the air freshens, let us go, why soon
The woodmen will be here; how we have lived this night of June!

Ave Imperatrix

Set in this stormy Northern sea,
    Queen of these restless fields of tide,
England! what shall men say of thee,
    Before whose feet the worlds divide?

The earth, a brittle globe of glass,
    Lies in the hollow of thy hand,
And through its heart of crystal pass,
    Like shadows through a twilight land,

The spears of crimson-suited war,
    The long white-crested waves of fight,   10
And all the deadly fires which are
    The torches of the lords of Night.

The yellow leopards, strained and lean,
    The treacherous Russian knows so well,
With gaping blackened jaws are seen
    Leap through the hail of screaming shell.

The strong sea-lion of England's wars
    Hath left his sapphire cave of sea,
To battle with the storm that mars
    The star of England's chivalry.   20

The brazen-throated clarion blows
　　Across the Pathan's reedy fen,
And the high steeps of Indian snows
　　Shake to the tread of armèd men.

And many an Afghan chief, who lies
　　Beneath his cool pomegranate-trees,
Clutches his sword in fierce surmise
　　When on the mountain-side he sees

The fleet-foot Marri scout, who comes
　　To tell how he hath heard afar　　　　　30
The measured roll of English drums
　　Beat at the gates of Kandahar.

For southern wind and east wind meet
　　Where, girt and crowned by sword and fire,
England with bare and bloody feet
　　Climbs the steep road of wide empire.

O lonely Himalayan height,
　　Grey pillar of the Indian sky,
Where saw'st thou last in clanging flight
　　Our wingèd dogs of Victory?　　　　　40

The almond-groves of Samarcand,
　　Bokhara, where red lilies blow,
And Oxus, by whose yellow sand
　　The grave white-turbaned merchants go:

And on from thence to Ispahan,
　　The gilded garden of the sun,
Whence the long dusty caravan
　　Brings cedar wood and vermilion;

And that dread city of Cabool
　　Set at the mountain's scarpèd feet,　　　50
Whose marble tanks are ever full
　　With water for the noonday heat:

Where through the narrow straight Bazaar
   A little maid Circassian
Is led, a present from the Czar
   Unto some old and bearded khan,—

Here have our wild war-eagles flown,
   And flapped wide wings in fiery fight;
But the sad dove, that sits alone
   In England—she hath no delight.   60

In vain the laughing girl will lean
   To greet her love with love-lit eyes:
Down in some treacherous black ravine,
   Clutching his flag, the dead boy lies.

And many a moon and sun will see
   The lingering wistful children wait
To climb upon their father's knee;
   And in each house made desolate

Pale women who have lost their lord
   Will kiss the relics of the slain—   70
Some tarnished epaulette—some sword—
   Poor toys to soothe such anguished pain.

For not in quiet English fields
   Are these, our brothers, lain to rest,
Where we might deck their broken shields
   With all the flowers the dead love best.

For some are by the Delhi walls,
   And many in the Afghan land,
And many where the Ganges falls
   Through seven mouths of shifting sand.   80

And some in Russian waters lie,
   And others in the seas which are
The portals to the East, or by
   The wind-swept heights of Trafalgar.

O wandering graves! O restless sleep!
   O silence of the sunless day!
O still ravine! O stormy deep!
   Give up your prey! give up your prey!

And thou whose wounds are never healed,
   Whose weary race is never won,   90
O Cromwell's England! must thou yield
   For every inch of ground a son?

Go! crown with thorns thy gold-crowned head,
   Change thy glad song to song of pain;
Wind and wild wave have got thy dead,
   And will not yield them back again.

Wave and wild wind and foreign shore
   Possess the flower of English land—
Lips that thy lips shall kiss no more,
   Hands that shall never clasp thy hand.   100

What profit now that we have bound
   The whole round world with nets of gold,
If hidden in our heart is found
   The care that groweth never old?

What profit that our galleys ride,
   Pine-forest-like, on every main?
Ruin and wreck are at our side,
   Grim warders of the House of pain.

Where are the brave, the strong, the fleet?
   Where is our English chivalry?   110
Wild grasses are their burial-sheet,
   And sobbing waves their threnody.

O loved ones lying far away,
   What word of love can dead lips send!
O wasted dust! O senseless clay!
   Is this the end! is this the end!

Peace, peace! we wrong the noble dead
  To vex their solemn slumber so;
Though childless, and with thorn-crowned head,
  Up the steep road must England go,   120

Yet when this fiery web is spun,
  Her watchmen shall descry from far
The young Republic like a sun
  Rise from these crimson seas of war.

Pan: Double Villanelle

I

O Goat-foot God of Arcady!
  This modern world is grey and old,
Ah what remains to us of Thee?

No more the shepherd lads in glee
  Throw apples at thy wattled fold,
O Goat-foot God of Arcady!

Nor through the laurels can one see
  Thy soft brown limbs, thy beard of gold,
Ah what remains to us of Thee?

And dull and dead our Thames would be   10
  For here the winds are chill and cold,
O Goat-foot God of Arcady!

Then keep the tomb of Helicé,
  Thine olive-woods, thy vine-clad wold,
Ah what remains to us of Thee?

Though many an unsung elegy
  Sleep in the reeds our rivers hold,
O Goat-foot God of Arcady!
Ah what remains to us of Thee?

II

Ah leave the hills of Arcady,   20
 Thy satyrs and their wanton play,
This modern world hath need of Thee.

No nymph or Faun indeed have we,
 For Faun and nymph are old and grey,
Ah leave the hills of Arcady!

This is the land where Liberty
 Lit grave-browed Milton on his way,
This modern world hath need of Thee!

A land of ancient chivalry
 Where gentle Sidney saw the day,   30
Ah leave the hills of Arcady!

This fierce sea-lion of the sea,
 This England, lacks some stronger lay,
This modern world hath need of Thee!

Then blow some Trumpet loud and free,
 And give thy oaten pipe away,
Ah leave the hills of Arcady!
This modern world hath need of Thee!

Sen Artysty; or, The Artist's Dream
(From the Polish of Madame Helena Modjeska)

I too have had my dreams: ay, known indeed
The crowded visions of a fiery youth
Which haunt me still.

         *   *   *   *

                    Methought that once I lay,
Within some garden-close, what time the Spring
Breaks like a bird from Winter, and the sky
Is sapphire-vaulted. The pure air was soft,

And the deep grass I lay on soft as air.
The strange and secret life of the young trees
Swelled in the green and tender bark, or burst
To buds of sheathèd emerald; violets   10
Peered from their nooks of hiding, half afraid
Of their own loveliness; the vermeil rose
Opened its heart, and the bright star-flower
Shone like a star of morning. Butterflies,
In painted liveries of brown and gold,
Took the shy bluebells as their pavilions
And seats of pleasaunce; overhead a bird
Made snow of all the blossoms as it flew
To charm the woods with singing: the whole world
Seemed waking to delight!
                    And yet—and yet—.   20
My soul was filled with leaden heaviness:
I had no joy in Nature; what to me,
Ambition's slave, was crimson-stainèd rose,
Or the gold-sceptred crocus? The bright bird
Sang out of tune for me, and the sweet flowers
Seemed but a pageant, and an unreal show
That mocked my heart; for, like the fabled snake
That stings itself to anguish, so I lay,
Self-tortured, self-tormented.
                        The day crept
Unheeded on the dial, till the sun   30
Dropt, purple-sailed, into the gorgeous East,
When, from the fiery heart of that great orb,
Came One whose shape of beauty far outshone
The most bright vision of this common earth.
Girt was she in a robe more white than flame,
Or furnace-heated brass; upon her head
She bare a laurel crown, and like a star
That falls from the high heaven suddenly,
Passed to my side.
                Then kneeling low, I cried,
'O much-desired! O long-waited for!   40
Immortal Glory! Great world-conqueror!
O let me not die crownless; once, at least,
Let thine imperial laurels bind my brows,
Ignoble else. Once let the clarion-note

And trump of loud ambition sound my name,
And for the rest I care not.'
                                    Then to me,
In gentle voice, the angel made reply:
'Child ignorant of the true happiness,
Nor knowing life's best wisdom, thou wert made
For light, and love, and laughter; not to waste   50
Thy youth in shooting arrows at the sun,
Or nurturing that ambition in thy soul
Whose deadly poison will infect thy heart,
Marring all joy and gladness! Tarry here,
In the sweet confines of this garden-close,
Whose level meads and glades delectable
Invite for pleasure; the wild bird that wakes
These silent dells with sudden melody
Shall be thy playmate; and each flower that blows
Shall twine itself unbidden in thy hair—   60
Garland more meet for thee than the dread weight
Of Glory's laurel-wreath.'
                              'Ah! fruitless gifts,'
I cried, unheeding of her prudent word,
'Are all such mortal flowers, whose brief lives
Are bounded by the dawn and setting sun.
The anger of the noon can wound the rose,
And the rain rob the crocus of its gold;
But thine immortal coronal of Fame,
Thy crown of deathless laurel, this alone
Age cannot harm, nor winter's icy tooth   70
Pierce to its hurt, nor common things profane.'
No answer made the angel, but her face
Dimmed with the mists of pity.
                                 Then methought
That from mine eyes, wherein ambition's torch
Burned with its latest and most ardent flame,
Flashed forth two level beams of straightened light,
Beneath whose fulgent fires the laurel crown
Twisted and curled, as when the Sirian star
Withers the ripening corn, and one pale leaf
Fell on my brow; and I leapt up and felt   80
The mighty pulse of Fame, and heard far off
The sound of many nations praising me!

*   *   *   *

One fiery-coloured moment of great life!
And then—how barren was the nations' praise!
How vain the trump of Glory! Bitter thorns
Were in that laurel leaf, whose toothèd barbs
Burned and bit deep till fire and red flame
Seemed to feed full upon my brain, and make
The garden a bare desert.
               With wild hands
I strove to tear it from my bleeding brow,   90
But all in vain; and with a dolorous cry
That paled the lingering stars before their time,
I waked at last, and saw the timorous dawn
Peer with grey face into my darkened room,
And would have deemed it a mere idle dream
But for this restless pain that gnaws my heart,
And the red wounds of thorns upon my brow.

Libertatis Sacra Fames

Albeit nurtured in democracy,
    And liking best that state republican
    Where every man is Kinglike and no man
Is crowned above his fellows, yet I see,
Spite of this modern fret for Liberty,
    Better the rule of One, whom all obey,
    Than to let clamorous demagogues betray
Our freedom with the kiss of anarchy.
Wherefore I love them not whose hands profane
    Plant the red flag upon the piled-up street   10
    For no right cause, beneath whose ignorant reign
Arts, Culture, Reverence, Honour, all things fade,
    Save Treason and the dagger of her trade,
    Or Murder with his silent bloody feet.

Sonnet to Liberty

Not that I love thy children, whose dull eyes
See nothing save their own unlovely woe,
Whose minds know nothing, nothing care to know,—
But that the roar of thy Democracies,
Thy reigns of Terror, thy great Anarchies,
Mirror my wildest passions like the sea
And give my rage a brother—! Liberty!
For this sake only do thy dissonant cries
Delight my discreet soul, else might all kings
By bloody knout or treacherous cannonades   10
Rob nations of their rights inviolate
And I remain unmoved—and yet, and yet,
These Christs that die upon the barricades,
God knows it I am with them, in some things.

Tædium Vitæ

To stab my youth with desperate knives, to wear
This paltry age's gaudy livery,
To let each base hand filch my treasury,
To mesh my soul within a woman's hair,
And be mere Fortune's lackeyed groom,—I swear
I love it not! these things are less to me
Than the thin foam that frets upon the sea,
Less than the thistle-down of summer air
Which hath no seed: better to stand aloof
Far from these slanderous fools who mock my life   10
Knowing me not, better the lowliest roof
Fit for the meanest hind to sojourn in,
Than to go back to that hoarse cave of strife
Where my white soul first kissed the mouth of sin.

Fabien dei Franchi

To My Friend Henry Irving

The silent room, the heavy creeping shade,
   The dead that travel fast, the opening door,
   The murdered brother rising through the floor,
The ghost's white fingers on thy shoulders laid,
And then the lonely duel in the glade,
   The broken swords, the stifled scream, the gore,
   Thy grand revengeful eyes when all is o'er,—
These things are well enough,—but thou wert made
   For more august creation! frenzied Lear
   Should at thy bidding wander on the heath   10
   With the shrill fool to mock him, Romeo
For thee should lure his love, and desperate fear
Pluck Richard's recreant dagger from its sheath—
   Thou trumpet set for Shakespeare's lips to blow!

Serenade

(For Music)

The western wind is blowing fair
   Across the dark Ægean sea,
And at the secret marble stair
   My Tyrian galley waits for thee.
Come down! the purple sail is spread,
   The watchman sleeps within the town,
O leave thy lily-flowered bed,
   O Lady mine come down, come down!

She will not come, I know her well,
   Of lover's vows she hath no care,   10
And little good a man can tell
   Of one so cruel and so fair.
True love is but a woman's toy,

They never know the lover's pain,
And I who loved as loves a boy
    Must love in vain, must love in vain.

O noble pilot tell me true
    Is that the sheen of golden hair?
Or is it but the tangled dew
    That binds the passion-flowers there?   20
Good sailor come and tell me now
    Is that my Lady's lily hand?
Or is it but the gleaming prow,
    Or is it but the silver sand?

No! no! 'tis not the tangled dew,
    'Tis not the silver-fretted sand,
It is my own dear Lady true
    With golden hair and lily hand!
O noble pilot steer for Troy,
    Good sailor ply the labouring oar,   30
This is the Queen of life and joy
    Whom we must bear from Grecian shore!

The waning sky grows faint and blue,
    It wants an hour still of day,
Aboard! aboard! my gallant crew,
    O Lady mine away! away!
O noble pilot steer for Troy,
    Good sailor ply the labouring oar,
O loved as only loves a boy!
    O loved for ever evermore!   40

Camma

As one who poring on a Grecian urn
    Scans the fair shapes some Attic hand hath made,
    God with slim goddess, goodly man with maid,
And for their beauty's sake is loth to turn
And face the obvious day, must I not yearn

For many a secret moon of indolent bliss,
  When in the midmost shrine of Artemis
I see thee standing, antique-limbed, and stern?

And yet—methinks I'd rather see thee play
  That serpent of old Nile, whose witchery   10
Made Emperors drunken,—come, great Egypt, shake
  Our stage with all thy mimic pageants! Nay,
  I am grown sick of unreal passions, make
The world thine Actium, me thine Antony!

Impression du Matin

The Thames nocturne of blue and gold
  Changed to a Harmony in grey:
  A barge with ochre-coloured hay
Dropt from the wharf: and chill and cold

The yellow fog came creeping down
  The bridges, till the houses' walls
  Seemed changed to shadows, and S. Paul's
Loomed like a bubble o'er the town.

Then suddenly arose the clang
  Of waking life; the streets were stirred   10
  With country waggons: and a bird
Flew to the glistening roofs and sang.

But one pale woman all alone,
  The daylight kissing her wan hair,
  Loitered beneath the gas lamps' flare,
With lips of flame and heart of stone.

In the Gold Room: A Harmony

Her ivory hands on the ivory keys
   Strayed in a fitful fantasy,
Like the silver gleam when the poplar trees
   Rustle their pale leaves listlessly,
Or the drifting foam of a restless sea
When the waves show their teeth in the flying breeze.

Her gold hair fell on the wall of gold
   Like the delicate gossamer tangles spun
On the burnished disk of the marigold,
   Or the sun-flower turning to meet the sun   10
   When the gloom of the dark blue night is done,
And the spear of the lily is aureoled.

And her sweet red lips on these lips of mine
   Burned like the ruby fire set
In the swinging lamp of a crimson shrine,
   Or the bleeding wounds of the pomegranate,
   Or the heart of the lotus drenched and wet
With the spilt-out blood of the rose-red wine.

Impressions

I

Les Silhouettes

The sea is flecked with bars of grey,
The dull dead wind is out of tune,
And like a withered leaf the moon
Is blown across the stormy bay.

Etched clear upon the pallid sand
Lies the black boat: a sailor boy
Clambers aboard in careless joy
With laughing face and gleaming hand.

And overhead the curlews cry,
Where through the dusky upland grass   10
The young brown-throated reapers pass,
Like silhouettes against the sky.

II

La Fuite de la Lune

To outer senses there is peace,
A dreamy peace on either hand,
Deep silence in the shadowy land,
Deep silence where the shadows cease.

Save for a cry that echoes shrill
From some lone bird disconsolate;
A corncrake calling to its mate;
The answer from the misty hill.

And suddenly the moon withdraws
Her sickle from the lightening skies,   10
And to her sombre cavern flies,
Wrapped in a veil of yellow gauze.

Impression
Le Réveillon

The sky is laced with fitful red,
The circling mists and shadows flee,
The dawn is rising from the sea,
Like a white lady from her bed.

And jagged brazen arrows fall
Athwart the feathers of the night,
And a long wave of yellow light
Breaks silently on tower and hall,

And spreading wide across the wold
Wakes into flight some fluttering bird,   10
And all the chestnut tops are stirred,
And all the branches streaked with gold.

Hélas!

To drift with every passion till my soul
Is a stringed lute on which all winds can play,
Is it for this that I have given away
Mine ancient wisdom, and austere control?
Methinks my life is a twice-written scroll
Scrawled over on some boyish holiday
With idle songs for pipe and virelay,
Which do but mar the secret of the whole.
Surely there was a time I might have trod
The sunlit heights, and from life's dissonance   10
Struck one clear chord to reach the ears of God:
Is that time dead? lo! with a little rod
I did but touch the honey of romance—
And must I lose a soul's inheritance?

Impressions

I

Le Jardin

The lily's withered chalice falls
    Around its rod of dusty gold,
    And from the beech trees on the wold
The last wood pigeon coos and calls.

The gaudy leonine sunflower
    Hangs black and barren on its stalk,
    And down the windy garden-walk
The dead leaves scatter,—hour by hour.

Pale privet-petals white as milk
   Are blown into a snowy mass: 10
   The roses lie upon the grass
Like little shreds of crimson silk.

II

La Mer

A white mist drifts across the shrouds,
   A wild moon in this wintry sky
   Gleams like an angry lion's eye
Out of a mane of tawny clouds.

The muffled steersman at the wheel
   Is but a shadow in the gloom;—
   And in the throbbing engine room
Leap the long rods of polished steel.

The shattered storm has left its trace
   Upon this huge and heaving dome,   10
   For the thin threads of yellow foam
Float on the waves like ravelled lace.

Le Jardin des Tuileries

This winter air is keen and cold,
   And keen and cold this winter sun,
   But round my chair the children run
Like little things of dancing gold.

Sometimes about the gaudy kiosk
   The mimic soldiers strut and stride,
   Sometimes the blue-eyed brigands hide
In the bleak tangles of the bosk.

And sometimes, while the old nurse cons
    Her book, they steal across the square,   10
    And launch their paper navies where
Huge Triton writhes in greenish bronze.

And now in mimic flight they flee,
    And now they rush, a boisterous band—
    And, tiny hand on tiny hand,
Climb up the black and leafless tree.

Ah! cruel tree! if I were you,
    And children climbed me, for their sake
    Though it be winter I would break
Into Spring blossoms white and blue!   20

The moon is like a yellow seal
    Upon a dark blue envelope;
    And soon below the dusky slope
Like a black sword of polished steel

With flickering damascenes of gold
    Lies the dim Seine, while here and there
    Flutters the white or crimson glare
Of some swift carriage homeward-rolled.

The Harlot's House

We caught the tread of dancing feet,
We loitered down the moonlit street,
And stopped beneath the Harlot's house.

Inside, above the din and fray,
We heard the loud musicians play
The 'Treues Liebes Herz' of Strauss.

Like strange mechanical grotesques,
Making fantastic arabesques,
The shadows raced across the blind.

We watched the ghostly dancers spin   10
To sound of horn and violin,
Like black leaves wheeling in the wind.

Like wire-pulled automatons,
Slim silhouetted skeletons
Went sidling through the slow quadrille,

Then took each other by the hand,
And danced a stately saraband;
Their laughter echoed thin and shrill.

Sometimes a clock-work puppet pressed
A phantom lover to her breast,   20
Sometimes they seemed to try and sing,

Sometimes a horrible Marionette
Came out, and smoked its cigarette
Upon the steps like a live thing.

Then turning to my love I said,
'The dead are dancing with the dead,
The dust is whirling with the dust.'

But she, she heard the violin,
And left my side, and entered in;
Love passed into the house of Lust.   30

Then suddenly the tune went false,
The dancers wearied of the waltz,
The shadows ceased to wheel and whirl,

And down the long and silent street,
The dawn with silver-sandalled feet,
Crept like a frightened girl.

Fantaisies Décoratives

I

Le Panneau

Under the rose-tree's dancing shade
 There stands a little ivory girl,
 Pulling the leaves of pink and pearl
With pale green nails of polished jade.

The red leaves fall upon the mould,
 The white leaves flutter, one by one,
 Down to a blue bowl where the sun,
Like a great dragon, writhes in gold.

The white leaves float upon the air,
 The red leaves flutter idly down,   10
 Some fall upon her yellow gown,
And some upon her raven hair.

She takes an amber lute and sings,
 And as she sings a silver crane
 Begins his scarlet neck to strain,
And flap his burnished metal wings.

She takes a lute of amber bright,
 And from the thicket where he lies
 Her lover, with his almond eyes,
Watches her movements in delight.   20

And now she gives a cry of fear,
 And tiny tears begin to start:
 A thorn has wounded with its dart
The pink-veined sea-shell of her ear.

And now she laughs a merry note:
  There has fallen a petal of the rose
  Just where the yellow satin shows
The blue-veined flower of her throat.

With pale green nails of polished jade,
  Pulling the leaves of pink and pearl,
  There stands a little ivory girl
Under the rose-tree's dancing shade.

II

Les Ballons

Against these turbid turquoise skies
  The light and luminous balloons
  Dip and drift like satin moons,
Drift like silken butterflies,

Reel with every windy gust,
  Rise and reel like dancing girls,
  Float like strange transparent pearls,
Fall and float like silver dust.

Now to the low leaves they cling,
  Each with coy fantastic pose,
  Each a petal of a rose
Straining at a gossamer string.

Then to the tall trees they climb,
  Like thin globes of amethyst,
  Wandering opals keeping tryst
With the rubies of the lime.

Under the Balcony

O beautiful star with the crimson mouth!
  O moon with the brows of gold!
Rise up, rise up, from the odorous south!
    And light for my love her way,
    Lest her little feet should stray
  On the windy hill and the wold!
O beautiful star with the crimson mouth!
  O moon with the brows of gold!

O ship that shakes on the desolate sea!
  O ship with the wet, white sail!   10
Put in, put in, to the port to me!
    For my love and I would go
    To the land where the daffodils blow
  In the heart of a violet dale!
O ship that shakes on the desolate sea!
  O ship with the wet, white sail!

O rapturous bird with the low, sweet note!
  O bird that sits on the spray!
Sing on, sing on, from your soft brown throat!
    And my love in her little bed   20
    Will listen, and lift her head
  From the pillow, and come my way!
O rapturous bird with the low, sweet note!
  O bird that sits on the spray!

O blossom that hangs in the tremulous air!
  O blossom with lips of snow!
Come down, come down, for my love to wear!
    You will die on her head in a crown,
    You will die in a fold of her gown,
  To her little light heart you will go!   30
O blossom that hangs in the tremulous air!
  O blossom with lips of snow!

To My Wife: With a Copy of My Poems

I can write no stately proem
  As a prelude to my lay;
From a poet to a poem
  I would dare to say.

For if of these fallen petals
  One to you seem fair,
Love will waft it till it settles
  On your hair.

And when wind and winter harden
  All the loveless land,   10
It will whisper of the garden,
  You will understand.

Sonnet
on the Sale by Auction of Keats' Love Letters

These are the letters which Endymion wrote
  To one he loved in secret, and apart.
  And now the brawlers of the auction mart
Bargain and bid for each poor blotted note,
Ay! for each separate pulse of passion quote
  The merchant's price: I think they love not Art
  Who break the crystal of a poet's heart
That small and sickly eyes may glare and gloat.

Is it not said that many years ago,
  In a far Eastern town, some soldiers ran
  With torches through the midnight, and began   10
To wrangle for mean raiment, and to throw
  Dice for the garments of a wretched man,
Not knowing the God's wonder, or His woe?

The New Remorse

The sin was mine; I did not understand.
  So now is music prisoned in her cave,
  Save where some ebbing desultory wave
Frets with its restless whirls this meagre strand.
And in the withered hollow of this land
  Hath Summer dug herself so deep a grave,
  That hardly can the leaden willow crave
One silver blossom from keen Winter's hand.
But who is this who cometh by the shore?
(Nay, love, look up and wonder!) Who is this   10
  Who cometh in dyed garments from the South?
It is thy new-found Lord, and he shall kiss
  The yet unravished roses of thy mouth,
And I shall weep and worship, as before.

Canzonet

I have no store
Of gryphon-guarded gold;
  Now, as before,
Bare is the shepherd's fold.
  Rubies, nor pearls,
Have I to gem thy throat;
  Yet woodland girls
Have loved the shepherd's note.

Then, pluck a reed
And bid me sing to thee,   10
  For I would feed
Thine ears with melody,
  Who art more fair
Than fairest fleur-de-lys,
  More sweet and rare
Than sweetest ambergris.

What dost thou fear?
Young Hyacinth is slain,
  Pan is not here,
And will not come again.   20
  No hornèd Faun
Treads down the yellow leas,
  No God at dawn
Steals through the olive trees.

  Hylas is dead,
Nor will he e'er divine
  Those little red
Rose-petalled lips of thine.
  On the high hill
No ivory Dryads play,   30
  Silver and still
Sinks the sad autumn day.

With a Copy of 'A House of Pomegranates'

Go, little book,
  To him who, on a lute with horns of pearl,
Sang of the white feet of the Golden Girl:
  And bid him look
Into thy pages: it may hap that he
May find that golden maidens dance through thee.

Symphony in Yellow

An omnibus across the bridge
  Crawls like a yellow butterfly,
  And, here and there, a passer-by
Shows like a little restless midge.

Big barges full of yellow hay
　　Are moored against the shadowy wharf,
　　And, like a yellow silken scarf,
The thick fog hangs along the quay.

The yellow leaves begin to fade
　　And flutter from the Temple elms,　　　　10
　　And at my feet the pale green Thames
Lies like a rod of rippled jade.

In the Forest

Out of the mid-wood's twilight
　　Into the meadow's dawn,
Ivory-limbed and brown-eyed
　　Flashes my Faun!

He skips through the copses singing,
　　And his shadow dances along,
And I know not which I should follow,
　　Shadow or song!

O Hunter, snare me his shadow!
　　O Nightingale, catch me his strain!　　　10
Else moonstruck with music and madness
　　I track him in vain.

The Sphinx

In a dim corner of my room for longer than my fancy thinks
A beautiful and silent Sphinx has watched me through the shifting
　　gloom.

Inviolate and immobile she does not rise she does not stir
For silver moons are naught to her and naught to her the suns that
　　reel.

Red follows grey across the air the waves of moonlight ebb and flow
But with the dawn she does not go and in the night-time she is
there.

Dawn follows dawn and nights grow old and all the while this
curious cat
Lies couching on the Chinese mat with eyes of satin rimmed with
gold.

Upon the mat she lies and leers and on the tawny throat of her
Flutters the soft and silky fur or ripples to her pointed ears.   10

Come forth my lovely seneschal! so somnolent, so statuesque!
Come forth you exquisite grotesque! half woman and half animal!

Come forth my lovely languorous Sphinx! and put your head upon
my knee!
And let me stroke your throat and see your body spotted like the
lynx!

And let me touch those curving claws of yellow ivory and grasp
The tail that like a monstrous asp coils round your heavy velvet
paws!

*

A thousand weary centuries are thine while I have hardly seen
Some twenty summers cast their green for autumn's gaudy liveries.

But you can read the hieroglyphs on the great sandstone obelisks,
And you have talked with Basilisks, and you have looked on
Hippogriffs.   20

O tell me, were you standing by when Isis to Osiris knelt?
And did you watch the Egyptian melt her union for Antony

And drink the jewel-drunken wine and bend her head in mimic
awe
To see the huge Proconsul draw the salted tunny from the brine?

And did you mark the Cyprian kiss white Adon on his catafalque?
And did you follow Amenalk, the god of Heliopolis?

And did you talk with Thoth, and did you hear the moon-horned
  Io weep?
And know the painted kings who sleep beneath the wedge-shaped
  pyramid?

*

Lift up your large black satin eyes which are like cushions where
  one sinks!
Fawn at my feet fantastic Sphinx! and sing me all your memories! 30

Sing to me of the Jewish maid who wandered with the Holy Child,
And how you led them through the wild, and how they slept
  beneath your shade.

Sing to me of that odorous green eve when couching by the marge
You heard from Adrian's gilded barge the laughter of Antinous

And lapped the stream and fed your drouth and watched with hot
  and hungry stare
The ivory body of that rare young slave with his pomegranate
  mouth!

Sing to me of the labyrinth in which the twy-formed Bull was
  stalled!
Sing to me of the night you crawled across the Temple's granite
  plinth

When through the purple corridors the screaming scarlet Ibis flew
In terror, and a horrid dew dripped from the moaning mandra-
  gores,
                                                              40

And the great torpid Crocodile within the tank shed slimy tears,
And tare the jewels from his ears and staggered back into the Nile,

And the priests cursed you with shrill psalms as in your claws you
  seized their Snake
And crept away with it to slake your passion by the shuddering
  palms!

*

Who were your lovers? who were they who wrestled for you in the
    dust?
Which was the vessel of your lust? what leman had you, every day?

Did giant Lizards come and crouch before you on the reedy banks?
Did Gryphons with great metal flanks leap on you in your trampled
    couch?

Did monstrous Hippopotami come sidling toward you in the mist?
Did gilt-scaled Dragons writhe and twist with passion as you
    passed them by?   50

And from the brick-built Lycian tomb what horrible Chimaera
    came
With fearful heads and fearful flame to breed new wonders from
    your womb?

*

Or had you shameful secret quests and did you harry to your home
Some Nereid coiled in amber foam with curious rock-crystal
    breasts?

Or did you treading through the froth call to the brown Sidonian
For tidings of Leviathan, Leviathan or Behemoth?

Or did you when the sun was set climb up the cactus-covered slope
To meet your swarthy Ethiop whose body was of polished jet?

Or did you while the earthen skiffs dropped down the grey Nilotic
    flats
At twilight and the flickering bats flew round the Temple's triple
    glyphs   60

Steal to the border of the bar and swim across the silent lake
And slink into the vault and make the pyramid your Lúpanar

Till from each black sarcophagus rose up the painted swathèd
    dead?
Or did you lure unto your bed the ivory-horned Tragelaphos?

Or did you love the God of Flies who plagued the Hebrews and was splashed
With wine unto the waist? or Pasht, who had green beryls for her eyes?

Or that young God, the Tyrian, who was more amorous than the dove
Or Ashtaroth? or did you love the God of the Assyrian

Whose wings, like strange transparent talc, rose high above his hawk-faced head,
Painted with silver and with red and ribbed with rods of orei-
chalch?   70

Or did huge Apis from his car leap down and lay before your feet
Big blossoms of the honey-sweet and honey-coloured nenuphar?

*

How subtle-secret is your smile! Did you love none then? Nay, I know
Great Ammon was your bedfellow! He lay with you beside the Nile!

The river-horses in the slime trumpeted when they saw him come
Odorous with Syrian galbanum and smeared with spikenard and with thyme.

He came along the river-bank like some tall galley argent-sailed,
He strode across the waters, mailed in beauty, and the waters sank.

He strode across the desert sand: he reached the valley where you lay:
He waited till the dawn of day: then touched your black breasts with his hand.   80

You kissed his mouth with mouths of flame: you made the hornèd God your own:
You stood behind him on his throne: you called him by his secret name.

You whispered monstrous oracles into the caverns of his ears:
With blood of goats and blood of steers you taught him monstrous
    miracles.

White Ammon was your bedfellow! Your chamber was the steam-
    ing Nile!
And with your curved archaic smile you watched his passion come
    and go.

                    *

With Syrian oils his brows were bright: and widespread as a tent at
    noon
His marble limbs made pale the moon and lent the day a larger
    light.

His long hair was nine cubits' span and coloured like that yellow
    gem
Which hidden in their garment's hem the merchants bring from
    Kurdistan.   90

His face was as the must that lies upon a vat of new-made wine:
The seas could not insapphirine the perfect azure of his eyes.

His thick soft throat was white as milk and threaded with thin veins
    of blue:
And curious pearls like frozen dew were broidered on his flowing
    silk.

                    *

On pearl and porphyry pedestalled he was too bright to look upon:
For on his ivory breast there shone the wondrous ocean-emerald,

That mystic moonlit jewel which some diver of the Colchian caves
Had found beneath the blackening waves and carried to the Col-
    chian witch.

Before his gilded galiot ran naked vine-wreathed Corybants,
And lines of swaying elephants knelt down to draw his chariot,   100

And lines of swarthy Nubians bare up his litter as he rode
Down the great granite-paven road between the nodding peacock-
    fans.

The merchants brought him steatite from Sidon in their painted
  ships:
The meanest cup that touched his lips was fashioned from a
  chrysolite.

The merchants brought him cedar-chests of rich apparel bound
  with cords:
His train was borne by Memphian Lords: young Kings were glad
  to be his guests.

Ten hundred shaven priests did bow to Ammon's altar day and
  night,
Ten hundred lamps did wave their light through Ammon's carven
  house—and now

Foul snake and speckled adder with their young ones crawl from
  stone to stone
For ruined is the house and prone the great rose-marble mono-
  lith!   110

Wild ass or trotting jackal comes and couches in the mouldering
  gates:
Wild satyrs call unto their mates across the fallen fluted drums

And on the summit of the pile the blue-faced ape of Horus sits
And gibbers while the figtree splits the pillars of the peristyle.

*

The god is scattered here and there: deep hidden in the windy sand
I saw his giant granite hand still clenched in impotent despair.

And many a wandering caravan of stately negroes silken-shawled,
Crossing the desert, halts appalled before the neck that none can
  span.

And many a bearded Bedouin draws back his yellow-striped
  burnous
To gaze upon the Titan thews of him who was thy paladin.   120

*

Go, seek his fragments on the moor and wash them in the evening dew,
And from their pieces make anew thy mutilated paramour!

Go, seek them where they lie alone and from their broken pieces make
Thy bruisèd bedfellow! and wake mad passions in the senseless stone!

Charm his dull ear with Syrian hymns! He loved your body! Oh, be kind,
Pour spikenard on his hair, and wind soft rolls of linen round his limbs!

Wind round his head the figured coins! Stain with red fruits those pallid lips!
Weave purple for his shrunken hips! and purple for his barren loins!

*

Away to Egypt! Have no fear. Only one God has ever died.   129
Only one God has let his side be wounded by a soldier's spear.

But these, thy lovers, are not dead. Still by the hundred-cubit gate
Dog-faced Anubis sits in state with lotus-lilies for thy head.

Still from his chair of porphyry gaunt Memnon strains his lidless eyes
Across the empty land, and cries each yellow morning unto Thee.

And Nilus with his broken horn lies in his black and oozy bed
And till thy coming will not spread his waters on the withering corn.

Your lovers are not dead, I know. They will rise up and hear your voice
And clash their cymbals and rejoice and run to kiss your mouth! And so,

Set wings upon your argosies! Set horses to your ebon car!
Back to your Nile! Or if you are grown sick of dead divinities   140

Follow some roving lion's spoor across the copper-coloured plain,
Reach out and hale him by the mane and bid him be your para-
mour!

Couch by his side upon the grass and set your white teeth in his
throat
And when you hear his dying note lash your long flanks of polished
brass

And take a tiger for your mate, whose amber sides are flecked with
black,
And ride upon his gilded back in triumph through the Theban
gate,

And toy with him in amorous jests, and when he turns, and snarls,
and gnaws,
O smite him with your jasper claws! and bruise him with your agate
breasts!

*

Why are you tarrying? Get hence! I weary of your sullen ways,
I weary of your steadfast gaze, your somnolent magnificence.   150

Your horrible and heavy breath makes the light flicker in the lamp,
And on my brow I feel the damp and dreadful dews of night and
death.

Your eyes are like fantastic moons that shiver in some stagnant lake,
Your tongue is like a scarlet snake that dances to fantastic tunes,

Your pulse makes poisonous melodies, and your black throat is like
the hole
Left by some torch or burning coal on Saracenic tapestries.

Away! the sulphur-coloured stars are hurrying through the
Western Gate!
Away! or it may be too late to climb their silent silver cars!

See, the dawn shivers round the grey gilt-dialled towers, and the
    rain
Streams down each diamonded pane and blurs with tears the
    wannish day.   160

What snake-tressed Fury fresh from Hell, with uncouth gestures
    and unclean,
Stole from the poppy-drowsy Queen and led you to a student's
    cell?

*

What songless tongueless ghost of Sin crept through the curtains
    of the night,
And saw my taper burning bright, and knocked, and bade you
    enter in.

Are there not others more accursed, whiter with leprosies than I?
Are Abana and Pharphar dry that you come here to slake your
    thirst?

Get hence, you loathsome Mystery! Hideous animal, get hence!
You wake in me each bestial sense, you make me what I would not
    be.

You make my creed a barren sham, you wake foul dreams of
    sensual life,
And Atys with his blood-stained knife were better than the thing I
    am.   170

False Sphinx! False Sphinx! By reedy Styx old Charon, leaning on
    his oar,
Waits for my coin. Go thou before, and leave me to my Crucifix,

Whose pallid burden, sick with pain, watches the world with
    wearied eyes,
And weeps for every soul that dies, and weeps for every soul in vain.

The Ballad of Reading Gaol

In Memoriam
C.T.W.
Sometime Trooper of the Royal Horse Guards.
Obiit HM Prison, Reading, Berkshire,
July 7th, 1896.

I

He did not wear his scarlet coat,
  For blood and wine are red,
And blood and wine were on his hands
  When they found him with the dead,
The poor dead woman whom he loved,
  And murdered in her bed.

He walked amongst the Trial Men
  In a suit of shabby gray;
A cricket cap was on his head,
  And his step seemed light and gay;   10
But I never saw a man who looked
  So wistfully at the day.

I never saw a man who looked
  With such a wistful eye
Upon that little tent of blue
  Which prisoners call the sky,
And at every drifting cloud that went
  With sails of silver by.

I walked, with other souls in pain,
  Within another ring,   20
And was wondering if the man had done
  A great or little thing,
When a voice behind me whispered low,
  'That fellow's got to swing.'

Dear Christ! the very prison walls
  Suddenly seemed to reel,

And the sky above my head became
   Like a casque of scorching steel;
And, though I was a soul in pain,
   My pain I could not feel.   30

I only knew what hunted thought
   Quickened his steps, and why
He looked upon the garish day
   With such a wistful eye;
The man had killed the thing he loved,
   And so he had to die.

*

Yet each man kills the thing he loves,
   By each let this be heard,
Some do it with a bitter look,
   Some with a flattering word,   40
The coward does it with a kiss,
   The brave man with a sword!

Some kill their love when they are young,
   And some when they are old;
Some strangle with the hands of Lust,
   Some with the hands of Gold:
The kindest use a knife, because
   The dead so soon grow cold.

Some love too little, some too long,
   Some sell, and others buy;   50
Some do the deed with many tears,
   And some without a sigh:
For each man kills the thing he loves,
   Yet each man does not die.

*

He does not die a death of shame
   On a day of dark disgrace,
Nor have a noose about his neck,
   Nor a cloth upon his face,

Nor drop feet foremost through the floor
  Into an empty space.   60

He does not sit with silent men
  Who watch him night and day;
Who watch him when he tries to weep,
  And when he tries to pray;
Who watch him lest himself should rob
  The prison of its prey.

He does not wake at dawn to see
  Dread figures throng his room,
The shivering Chaplain robed in white,
  The Sheriff stern with gloom,   70
And the Governor all in shiny black,
  With the yellow face of Doom.

He does not rise in piteous haste
  To put on convict-clothes,
While some coarse-mouthed Doctor gloats, and notes
  Each new and nerve-twitched pose,
Fingering a watch whose little ticks
  Are like horrible hammer-blows.

He does not know that sickening thirst
  That sands one's throat, before   80
The hangman with his gardener's gloves
  Slips through the padded door,
And binds one with three leathern thongs,
  That the throat may thirst no more.

He does not bend his head to hear
  The Burial Office read,
Nor, while the terror of his soul
  Tells him he is not dead,
Cross his own coffin, as he moves
  Into the hideous shed.   90

He does not stare upon the air
  Through a little roof of glass:
He does not pray with lips of clay
  For his agony to pass;
Nor feel upon his shuddering cheek
  The kiss of Caiaphas.

ii

Six weeks our guardsman walked the yard,
  In the suit of shabby gray:
His cricket cap was on his head,
  And his step seemed light and gay,   100
But I never saw a man who looked
  So wistfully at the day.

I never saw a man who looked
  With such a wistful eye
Upon that little tent of blue
  Which prisoners call the sky,
And at every wandering cloud that trailed
  Its ravelled fleeces by.

He did not wring his hands, as do
  Those witless men who dare   110
To try to rear the changeling Hope
  In the cave of black Despair:
He only looked upon the sun,
  And drank the morning air.

He did not wring his hands nor weep,
  Nor did he peek or pine,
But he drank the air as though it held
  Some healthful anodyne;
With open mouth he drank the sun
  As though it had been wine!   120

And I and all the souls in pain,
  Who tramped the other ring,

Forgot if we ourselves had done
　　A great or little thing,
And watched with gaze of dull amaze
　　The man who had to swing.

And strange it was to see him pass
　　With a step so light and gay,
And strange it was to see him look
　　So wistfully at the day,　　　　　　　　　130
And strange it was to think that he
　　Had such a debt to pay.

*

For oak and elm have pleasant leaves
　　That in the spring-time shoot:
But grim to see is the gallows-tree,
　　With its adder-bitten root,
And, green or dry, a man must die
　　Before it bears its fruit!

The loftiest place is that seat of grace
　　For which all worldlings try:　　　　　　140
But who would stand in hempen band
　　Upon a scaffold high,
And through a murderer's collar take
　　His last look at the sky?

It is sweet to dance to violins
　　When Love and Life are fair:
To dance to flutes, to dance to lutes
　　Is delicate and rare:
But it is not sweet with nimble feet
　　To dance upon the air!　　　　　　　　　150

So with curious eyes and sick surmise
　　We watched him day by day,
And wondered if each one of us
　　Would end the self-same way,

For none can tell to what red Hell
   His sightless soul may stray.

                *

At last the dead man walked no more
   Amongst the Trial Men,
And I knew that he was standing up
   In the black dock's dreadful pen,   160
And that never would I see his face
   In God's sweet world again.

Like two doomed ships that pass in storm
   We had crossed each other's way:
But we made no sign, we said no word,
   We had no word to say;
For we did not meet in the holy night,
   But in the shameful day.

A prison wall was round us both,
   Two outcast men we were: 170
The world had thrust us from its heart,
   And God from out His care:
And the iron gin that waits for Sin
   Had caught us in its snare.

iii

In Debtor's Yard the stones are hard,
   And the dripping wall is high,
So it was there he took the air
   Beneath the leaden sky,
And by each side a Warder walked,
   For fear the man might die.   180

Or else he sat with those who watched
   His anguish night and day;
Who watched him when he rose to weep,
   And when he crouched to pray;
Who watched him lest himself should rob
   Their scaffold of its prey.

The Governor was strong upon
  The Regulations Act:
The Doctor said that Death was but
  A scientific fact: 190
And twice a day the Chaplain called,
  And left a little tract.

And twice a day he smoked his pipe,
  And drank his quart of beer:
His soul was resolute, and held
  No hiding-place for fear;
He often said that he was glad
  The hangman's hands were near.

But why he said so strange a thing
  No Warder dared to ask: 200
For he to whom a watcher's doom
  Is given as his task,
Must set a lock upon his lips,
  And make his face a mask.

Or else he might be moved, and try
  To comfort or console:
And what should Human Pity do
  Pent up in Murderers' Hole?
What word of grace in such a place
  Could help a brother's soul?   210

*

With slouch and swing around the ring
  We trod the Fools' Parade!
We did not care: we knew we were
  The Devil's Own Brigade:
And shaven head and feet of lead
  Make a merry masquerade.

We tore the tarry rope to shreds
  With blunt and bleeding nails;

We rubbed the doors, and scrubbed the floors,
　　And cleaned the shining rails:　　　　220
And, rank by rank, we soaped the plank,
　　And clattered with the pails.

We sewed the sacks, we broke the stones,
　　We turned the dusty drill:
We banged the tins, and bawled the hymns,
　　And sweated on the mill:
But in the heart of every man
　　Terror was lying still.

So still it lay that every day
　　Crawled like a weed-clogged waved:　　230
And we forgot the bitter lot
　　That waits for fool and knave,
Till once, as we tramped in from work,
　　We passed an open grave.

With yawning mouth the yellow hole
　　Gaped for a living thing;
The very mud cried out for blood
　　To the thirsty asphalte ring:
And we knew that ere one dawn grew fair
　　Some prisoner had to swing.　　　　240

Right in we went, with soul intent
　　On Death and Dread and Doom:
The hangman, with his little bag,
　　Went shuffling through the gloom:
And each man trembled as he crept
　　Into his numbered tomb.

*

That night the empty corridors
　　Were full of forms of Fear,
And up and down the iron town
　　Stole feet we could not hear,　　　　250

And through the bars that hide the stars
　　White faces seemed to peer.

He lay as one who lies and dreams
　　In a pleasant meadow-land,
The watchers watched him as he slept,
　　And could not understand
How one could sleep so sweet a sleep
　　With a hangman close at hand.

But there is no sleep when men must weep
　　Who never yet have wept: 260
So we—the fool, the fraud, the knave—
　　That endless vigil kept,
And through each brain on hands of pain
　　Another's terror crept.

*

Alas! it is a fearful thing
　　To feel another's guilt!
For, right within, the sword of Sin
　　Pierced to its poisoned hilt,
And as molten lead were the tears we shed
　　For the blood we had not spilt.   270

The Warders with their shoes of felt
　　Crept by each padlocked door,
And peeped and saw, with eyes of awe,
　　Gray figures on the floor,
And wondered why men knelt to pray
　　Who never prayed before.

All through the night we knelt and prayed,
　　Mad mourners of a corse!
The troubled plumes of midnight were
　　The plumes upon a hearse: 280
And bitter wine upon a sponge
　　Was the savour of Remorse.

*

The gray cock crew, the red cock crew,
    But never came the day:
And crooked shapes of Terror crouched,
    In the corners where we lay:
And each evil sprite that walks by night
    Before us seemed to play.

They glided past, they glided fast,
    Like travellers through a mist: 290
They mocked the moon in a rigadoon
    Of delicate turn and twist,
And with formal pace and loathsome grace
    The phantoms kept their tryst.

With mop and mow, we saw them go,
    Slim shadows hand in hand:
About, about, in ghostly rout
    They trod a saraband:
And the damned grotesques made arabesques,
    Like the wind upon the sand!   300

With the pirouettes of marionettes,
    They tripped on pointed tread:
But with flutes of Fear they filled the ear,
    As their grisly masque they led,
And loud they sang, and long they sang,
    For they sang to wake the dead.

'Oho!' they cried, 'The world is wide,
    But fettered limbs go lame!
And once, or twice, to throw the dice
    Is a gentlemanly game,   310
But he does not win who plays with Sin
    In the secret House of Shame.'

                    *

No things of air these antics were,
    That frolicked with such glee:
To men whose lives were held in gyves,

And whose feet might not go free,
Ah! wounds of Christ! they were living things,
    Most terrible to see.

Around, around, they waltzed and wound;
    Some wheeled in smirking pairs;   320
With the mincing step of a demirep
    Some sidled up the stairs:
And with subtle sneer, and fawning leer,
    Each helped us at our prayers.

                    *

The morning wind began to moan,
    But still the night went on:
Through its giant loom the web of gloom
    Crept till each thread was spun:
And, as we prayed, we grew afraid
    Of the Justice of the Sun.   330

The moaning wind went wandering round
    The weeping prison-wall:
Till like a wheel of turning steel
    We felt the minutes crawl:
O moaning wind! what had we done
    To have such a seneschal?

At last I saw the shadowed bars,
    Like a lattice wrought in lead,
Move right across the whitewashed wall
    That faced my three-plank bed,   340
And I knew that somewhere in the world
    God's dreadful dawn was red.

                    *

At six o'clock we cleaned our cells,
    At seven all was still,
But the sough and swing of a mighty wing
    The prison seemed to fill,
For the Lord of Death with icy breath
    Had entered in to kill.

He did not pass in purple pomp,
   Nor ride a moon-white steed.   350
Three yards of cord and a sliding board
   Are all the gallows' need:
So with rope of shame the Herald came
   To do the secret deed.

*

We were as men who through a fen
   Of filthy darkness grope:
We did not dare to breathe a prayer,
   Or to give our anguish scope:
Something was dead in each of us,
   And what was dead was Hope.   360

For Man's grim Justice goes its way,
   And will not swerve aside:
It slays the weak, it slays the strong,
   It has a deadly stride:
With iron heel it slays the strong,
   The monstrous parricide!

*

We waited for the stroke of eight:
   Each tongue was thick with thirst:
For the stroke of eight is the stroke of Fate
   That makes a man accursed,   370
And Fate will use a running noose
   For the best man and the worst.

We had no other thing to do,
   Save to wait for the sign to come:
So, like things of stone in a valley lone,
   Quiet we sat and dumb:
But each man's heart beat thick and quick,
   Like a madman on a drum!

*

With sudden shock the prison-clock
   Smote on the shivering air,   380
And from all the gaol rose up a wail

Of impotent despair,
Like the sound that frightened marshes hear
    From some leper in his lair.

And as one sees most fearful things
    In the crystal of a dream,
We saw the greasy hempen rope
    Hooked to the blackened beam,
And heard the prayer the hangman's snare
    Strangled into a scream.   390

And all the woe that moved him so
    That he gave that bitter cry,
And the wild regrets, and the bloody sweats,
    None knew so well as I:
For he who lives more lives than one
    More deaths than one must die.

                    IV

There is no chapel on the day
    On which they hang a man:
The Chaplain's heart is far too sick,
    Or his face is far too wan,   400
Or there is that written in his eyes
    Which none should look upon.

So they kept us close till nigh on noon,
    And then they rang the bell,
And the Warders with their jingling keys
    Opened each listening cell,
And down the iron stair we tramped,
    Each from his separate Hell.

Out into God's sweet air we went,
    But not in wonted way,   410
For this man's face was white with fear,
    And that man's face was gray,
And I never saw sad men who looked
    So wistfully at the day.

I never saw sad men who looked
    With such a wistful eye
Upon that little tent of blue
    We prisoners called the sky,
And at every careless cloud that passed
    In happy freedom by.   420

But there were those amongst us all
    Who walked with downcast head,
And knew that, had each got his due,
    They should have died instead;
He had but killed a thing that lived,
    Whilst they had killed the dead.

For he who sins a second time
    Wakes a dead soul to pain,
And draws it from its spotted shroud,
    And makes it bleed again,   430
And makes it bleed great gouts of blood,
    And makes it bleed in vain!

                        *

Like ape or clown, in monstrous garb
    With crooked arrows starred,
Silently we went round and round
    The slippery asphalte yard;
Silently we went round and round,
    And no man spoke a word.

Silently we went round and round,
    And through each hollow mind   440
The Memory of dreadful things
    Rushed like a dreadful wind,
And Horror stalked before each man,
    And Terror crept behind.

                        *

The Warders strutted up and down,
    And kept their herd of brutes,
Their uniforms were spick and span,

And they wore their Sunday suits,
But we knew the work they had been at,
    By the quicklime on their boots.   450

For where a grave had opened wide,
    There was no grave at all:
Only a stretch of mud and sand
    By the hideous prison-wall,
And a little heap of burning lime,
    That the man should have his pall.

For he has a pall, this wretched man,
    Such as few men can claim:
Deep down below a prison-yard,
    Naked for greater shame,   460
He lies, with fetters on each foot,
    Wrapt in a sheet of flame!

And all the while the burning lime
    Eats flesh and bone away,
It eats the brittle bone by night,
    And the soft flesh by day,
It eats the flesh and bone by turns,
    But it eats the heart alway.

                    *

For three long years they will not sow
    Or root or seedling there: 470
For three long years the unblessed spot
    Will sterile be and bare,
And look upon the wondering sky
    With unreproachful stare.

They think a murderer's heart would taint
    Each simple seed they sow.
It is not true! God's kindly earth
    Is kindlier than men know,
And the red rose would but blow more red,
    The white rose whiter blow.   480

Out of his mouth a red, red rose!
   Out of his heart a white!
For who can say by what strange way,
   Christ brings His will to light,
Since the barren staff the pilgrim bore
   Bloomed in the great Pope's sight?

*

But neither milk-white rose nor red
   May bloom in prison air;
The shard, the pebble, and the flint,
   Are what they give us there:
For flowers have been known to heal   490
   A common man's despair.

So never will wine-red rose or white,
   Petal by petal, fall
On that stretch of mud and sand that lies
   By the hideous prison-wall,
To tell the men who tramp the yard
   That God's Son died for all.

*

Yet though the hideous prison-wall
   Still hems him round and round,   500
And a spirit may not walk by night
   That is with fetters bound,
And a spirit may but weep that lies
   In such unholy ground,

He is at peace—this wretched man—
   At peace, or will be soon:
There is no thing to make him mad,
   Nor does Terror walk at noon,
For the lampless Earth in which he lies
   Has neither Sun nor Moon.   510

*

They hanged him as a beast is hanged:
   They did not even toll
A requiem that might have brought

Rest to his startled soul,
But hurriedly they took him out,
  And hid him in a hole.

They stripped him of his canvas clothes,
  And gave him to the flies:
They mocked the swollen purple throat,
  And the stark and staring eyes: 520
And with laughter loud they heaped the shroud
  In which their convict lies.

The Chaplain would not kneel to pray
  By his dishonoured grave:
Nor mark it with that blessed Cross
  That Christ for sinners gave,
Because the man was one of those
  Whom Christ came down to save.

Yet all is well; he has but passed
  To Life's appointed bourne: 530
And alien tears will fill for him
  Pity's long-broken urn,
For his mourners will be outcast men,
  And outcasts always mourn.

V

I know not whether Laws be right,
  Or whether Laws be wrong;
All that we know who lie in gaol
  Is that the wall is strong;
And that each day is like a year,
  A year whose days are long.   540

But this I know, that every Law
  That men have made for Man,
Since first Man took his brother's life,
  And the sad world began,
But straws the wheat and saves the chaff
  With a most evil fan.

This too I know—and wise it were
　If each could know the same—
That every prison that men build
　Is built with bricks of shame,
And bound with bars lest Christ should see
　How men their brothers maim.

With bars they blur the gracious moon,
　And blind the goodly sun:
And they do well to hide their Hell,
　For in it things are done
That Son of God nor son of Man
　Ever should look upon!

*

The vilest deeds like poison weeds
　Bloom well in prison-air:
It is only what is good in Man
　That wastes and withers there:
Pale Anguish keeps the heavy gate,
　And the Warder is Despair.

For they starve the little frightened child
　Till it weeps both night and day:
And they scourge the weak, and flog the fool,
　And gibe the old and gray,
And some grow mad, and all grow bad,
　And none a word may say.

Each narrow cell in which we dwell
　Is a foul and dark latrine,
And the fetid breath of living Death
　Chokes up each grated screen,
And all, but Lust, is turned to dust
　In Humanity's machine.

The brackish water that we drink
　Creeps with a loathsome slime,
And the bitter bread they weigh in scales

Is full of chalk and lime,   580
And Sleep will not lie down, but walks
  Wild-eyed, and cries to Time.

                    *

But though lean Hunger and green Thirst
  Like asp with adder fight,
We have little care of prison fare,
  For what chills and kills outright
Is that every stone one lifts by day
  Becomes one's heart by night.

With midnight always in one's heart,
  And twilight in one's cell,   590
We turn the crank, or tear the rope,
  Each in his separate Hell,
And the silence is more awful far
  Than the sound of a brazen bell.

And never a human voice comes near
  To speak a gentle word:
And the eye that watches through the door
  Is pitiless and hard:
And by all forgot, we rot and rot,
  With soul and body marred.   600

And thus we rust Life's iron chain
  Degraded and alone:
And some men curse, and some men weep,
  And some men make no moan:
But God's eternal Laws are kind
  And break the heart of stone.

                    *

And every human heart that breaks,
  In prison-cell or yard,
Is as that broken box that gave
  Its treasure to the Lord,   610
And filled the unclean leper's house
  With the scent of costliest nard.

Ah! happy they whose hearts can break
  And peace of pardon win!
How else may man make straight his plan
  And cleanse his soul from Sin?
How else but through a broken heart
  May Lord Christ enter in?

                    *

And he of the swollen purple throat,
  And the stark and staring eyes,   620
Waits for the holy hands that took
  The Thief to Paradise;
And a broken and a contrite heart
  The Lord will not despise.

The man in red who reads the Law
  Gave him three weeks of life,
Three little weeks in which to heal
  His soul of his soul's strife,
And cleanse from every blot of blood
  The hand that held the knife.   630

And with tears of blood he cleansed the hand,
  The hand that held the steel:
For only blood can wipe out blood,
  And only tears can heal:
And the crimson stain that was of Cain
  Became Christ's snow-white seal.

                   VI

In Reading gaol by Reading town
  There is a pit of shame,
And in it lies a wretched man
  Eaten by teeth of flame,   640
In a burning winding-sheet he lies,
  And his grave has got no name.

And there, till Christ call forth the dead,
  In silence let him lie:
No need to waste the foolish tear,

Or heave the windy sigh:
The man had killed the thing he loved,
And so he had to die.

And all men kill the thing they love,
By all let this be heard,   650
Some do it with a bitter look,
Some with a flattering word,
The coward does it with a kiss,
The brave man with a sword!

C. 3. 3.

APPENDIX

Wilde's Ordering of Poems (1882)

Hélas!

Eleutheria:
    Sonnet to Liberty
    Ave Imperatrix
    To Milton
    Louis Napoleon
    Sonnet on the Massacre of the Christians in Bulgaria
    Quantum Mutata
    Libertatis Sacra Fames
    Theoretikos

The Garden of Eros

Rosa Mystica:
    Requiescat
    Sonnet on Approaching Italy
    San Miniato
    Ave Maria Plena Gratia
    Italia
    Sonnet Written in Holy Week at Genoa
    Rome Unvisited
    Urbs Sacra Æterna
    Sonnet on Hearing the Dies Iræ Sung in the Sistine Chapel
    Easter Day
    E Tenebris
    Vita Nuova
    Madonna Mia
    The New Helen

The Burden of Itys

Wind Flowers:
    Impression du Matin
    Magdalen Walks
    Athanasia
    Serenade
    Endymion
    La Bella Donna Della Mia Mente
    Chanson

Charmides

Flowers of Gold:
    Impressions: I. Les Silhouettes
                          II. La Fuite de la Lune
    The Grave of Keats
    Theocritus: A Villanelle
    In the Gold Room: A Harmony
    Ballade de Marguerite
    The Dole of the King's Daughter
    Amor Intellectualis
    Santa Decca
    A Vision
    Impression de Voyage
    The Grave of Shelley
    By the Arno

Impressions de Theatre:
    Fabien dei Franchi
    Phèdre
    Sonnets Written at the Lyceum Theatre:
        I. Portia
        II. Queen Henrietta Maria
    Camma

Panthea

The Fourth Movement:
    Impression: Le Réveillon
    At Verona
    Apologia
    Quia Multum Amavi
    Silentium Amoris
    Her Voice
    My Voice
    Tædium Vitæ

Humanitad

Flower of Love:
    Γλυκύπικρος ἔρως

Notes

These notes have been kept to a minimum, and there is no attempt to indicate sources of influence in the early poems, or to gloss every place-name, whether in Oxfordshire or in Italy and Greece. The early poems are very taken up with ancient mythology. Wilde uses Greek and Latin deities interchangeably, depending on mood or metre at the time. Very common words such as Hellenic, Attic, Arcady, and Castaly, sacred to Apollo and the muses, are not glossed.

Greek titles are glossed on the page, other foreign titles and epigraphs generally in the Notes. Besides Fong's 'The Poetry of Oscar Wilde: A Critical Edition', Ph.D. thesis, University of California, Los Angeles (1978), other texts occasionally referred to include: Rupert Hart-Davis (ed.), *Letters of Oscar Wilde* (1962) and *More Letters of Oscar Wilde* (1985); Isobel Murray (ed.), The Oxford Authors *Oscar Wilde* (1989) and *The Soul of Man and Prison Writings* (1990); Robert Ross (ed.), *Miscellanies* in his collected edition of Wilde (1908); and Philip E. Smith II and Michael S. Helfand (eds.), *Oscar Wilde's Oxford Notebooks* (1989).

1 *Chorus of Cloud-Maidens*. A free translation of two songs (denoted 'strophe' and 'antistrophe' in the poem) from Aristophanes' *The Clouds*. The chorus would sing the strophe as it moved towards one side, answered by its exact counterpart as it returned.

   l. 16. *Pallas-loved land*: Athens.

   l. 18. *Kekrops*: legendary first king of Attica and founder of Athens.

3 *Requiescat*: may she rest. Said to have been written in memory of Wilde's younger sister Isola, who died, aged 8, in 1867.

4 *San Miniato*. Hill in Florence.

   l. 2. *house of God*: romanesque church of San Miniato al Monte.

   l. 3. *Angel-Painter*: fifteenth-century painter known as Fra Angelico. (Typically Wildean casual treatment of fact: Fra Angelico's works are in the Dominican monastery of San Marco.)

4 *By the Arno*. The river on which Florence stands.

5 *Rome Unvisited*. See *More Letters*, 23.

   ll. 9, 11, 13. *Blessed Lady . . . Mother . . . Roma*: Rome.

   l. 12. *triple gold*: the papal tiara.

6 ll. 20–4. *Fiesole . . . Apennines*: the region round Florence visited by Wilde during his Italian tour, 1875.

6 l. 27. *drear Campagna*: 'drear' perhaps because of the marshes surrounding Rome.

l. 28. *dome*: St Peter's Basilica, Rome.

l. 32. *awful keys*: the pope. Matthew 16: 19: Christ gave Peter, the first pope, the keys of the kingdom of heaven.

7 *La Bella Donna Della Mia Mente*: lovely Lady of my Memory. Dante had called Beatrice 'Glorious lady of my memory'.

8 l. 21. *melilote*: a clover-like grass.

10 Αἴλινον, αἴλινον εἰπέ, τὸ δ' εὖ νικάτω. From Aeschylus' *Agamemnon*, 121. For strophe and antistrophe see headnote to 'Chorus of Cloud-Maidens'.

l. 12. *ladders*: cf. Genesis 28: 12.

11 *The True Knowledge*. Possibly inspired by the death of Wilde's father, Sir William Wilde, in 1876. Epigraph: from a fragment of Euripides' play *Hypsipile*.

11 Θρηνῳδία. Translation of a choral song from Euripides' *Hecuba*. For strophe and antistrophe see headnote to 'Chorus of Cloud-Maidens'.

12 l. 17. *distant shore*: Delos, the central island of the Kyklades group in the Aegean, where the Titaness Leto, pregnant by Zeus, gave birth to Apollo and Artemis.

14 *Lotus Leaves*. In Homer's *Odyssey* the effect of eating the lotus was to make people forget their families, and live in ease, luxury, and idleness. Like 'The True Knowledge', this poem may have been inspired by the death of Sir William Wilde in 1876. Epigraph: from Homer's *Odyssey*, iv. 195–8. Peistratus speaks when Telemachus laments his father Odysseus, feared dead.

17 *A Fragment from the Agamemnon of Aeschylos*. Apollo, in love with Kasandra, had given her the gift of prophecy. But when she rejected his advances, he cursed the gift so that her prophecies were never believed.

ll. 5–8. See headnote to 'The Burden of Itys'.

18 l. 23. *bridegroom*: Paris, whose abduction of Helen began the Trojan War.

19 l. 29. *dark land*: the kingdom of Hades with the river Acheron and its tributary Kokutos.

l. 45. *my Sire*: Priam, king of Troy.

20 *A Vision*. Euripides was a favourite author of Wilde the student. See *Letters* 51, 59; and *Commonplace Book*, 132, 'the great humanist of

Hellas, the cor cordium of antiquity' (in Smith and Helfand, *Oscar Wilde's Oxford Notebooks*).

ll. 1–2. Of the three ancient Greek masters of tragedy, Aeschylus and Sophocles were frequent victors at the annual Dionysian dramatic competitions, but Euripides, whose plays provocatively criticized contemporary institutions, seldom won the crown of laurel wreaths.

l. 8. *broken stone*. In legend, Euripides' cenotaph was struck by lightning, a sign of the gods' displeasure.

l. 11. *Beatricé*. In parts of Dante's *Purgatorio* and *Paradiso*, his honoured lady acts as his guide.

20 *Sonnet on Approaching Italy*.

l. 13. *second Peter*. Pope Pius IX refused to recognize the united kingdom of Italy, which had wrested Rome from ecclesiastical control in 1871. He considered himself 'imprisoned' in the Vatican.

22 *The Theatre at Argos*.

l. 2. *crowned with olive*. The olive was sacred to Athena, and a crown was the highest distinction for a citizen, and the highest prize in the Olympic Games.

l. 7. *Danae*. Acrisius, king of Argos, imprisoned his daughter Danae underground, because of a prophecy that she would bear a son who would kill him. Zeus visited her in a shower of gold and impregnated her with her son, Perseus, who did accidentally kill Acrisius.

22 *Urbs Sacra Æterna*. Sacred and Eternal City.

ll. 8–14. *hated flag . . . prisoned shepherd*. See 'Sonnet on Approaching Italy', l. 13.

23 *The Grave of Keats*. In the Protestant Cemetery at Rome. Cf. the prose account in *Miscellanies*, 1–4.

l. 4. Keats died of tuberculosis at 24.

l. 5. *Sebastian*. Wilde much admired Guido Reni's painting of the young Sebastian, pierced by arrows, and after prison took this for his first name. Sebastian is a favourite saint among homosexuals.

l. 10. *Mitylene*: chief city of Lesbos, home of the poets Sappho and Alcaeus in the sixth century BC.

l. 12. *writ in water*: Keats asked for his epitaph to read: 'Here lies one whose name was writ in water'.

l. 14. *Isabella*. Cf. Keats's poem 'Isabella; or, The Pot of Basil', where the woman keeps her murdered lover's head in a pot of basil, which grows green with her tears.

23 *Sonnet on the Massacre of the Christians in Bulgaria*. In May 1876 occurred one in a series of Turkish atrocities that inflamed the

Balkans. Obviously modelled after Milton's sonnet 'On the Late Massacre in Piedmont'.

23 *l. 3. Her*: cf. Luke 7: 47. Wilde regularly identified the woman whose sins were forgiven because 'she loved much' as Mary Magdalene, first to see Christ after the Resurrection (John 20: 15–17).

l. 11. *Crescent*: Muslim symbol.

ll. 12–13. Cf. Matthew 27: 40.

24 *Easter Day*.

l. 1. *Dome*: St Peter's, Rome.

l. 7. *Three crowns*: the papal tiara.

l. 11. Cf. Luke 9: 58.

l. 14. Cf. Genesis 3: 15.

24 *Sonnet on Hearing the Dies Iræ Sung in the Sistine Chapel*. 'Dies Iræ' is 'The Day of Wrath', traditional sequence from the Roman Catholic Mass of Interment of the Dead. Wilde's poem rejects the traditional belief that at the Judgement, heaven and earth will pass away in fire.

l. 7. Cf. Luke 9: 58.

25 *Italia*.

l. 8. *one flag*: see 'Sonnet on Approaching Italy', l. 13 n.

25 *Vita Nuova*: The New Life. Copying Dante's title for his visionary poem and apologia. Cf. *Letters*, 475.

l. 13. *white limbs*: Venus, who was born from the foam of the sea.

26 *E Tenebris*. Out of Darkness. Some Roman Catholic Holy Week services were known as Tenebrae, where darkness eclipsed the Light of the World. See also e.g. Psalm 107: 10, Matthew 22: 13.

ll. 2–3. Cf. Matthew 14.

l. 4. *wine of life*. Cf. *Macbeth* II. iii. 102, 'The wine of life is drawn', and *Letters*, 384, 'On the sand is my life spilt'.

l. 10. *Baal*. The prophet Elijah taunted the priests of Baal for their god's impotence: 1 Kings 18: 27.

l. 13. *feet of brass*. Cf. Revelation 1: 14–15. Also a reference to the statue of Peter in St Peter's, Rome.

26 *Quantum Mutata*. How much Changed. Cf. Virgil, *Aeneid* ii. 274. Cf. 'Sonnet on the Massacre of the Christians in Bulgaria'.

ll. 6–9. In 1655 the Waldensian sect were harried from their homes in Piedmont. Pope Alexander VII did not object, but Cromwell summoned the Protestant powers and forced restitution to the surviving Waldenses.

27 *To Milton*. Cf. Wordsworth's 'Milton! Thou shouldst be living at this hour'.

ll. 10. *sea-lion*: in heraldry, a lion terminating in a fish's tail. It combines the traditional symbol of England with an allusion to the naval supremacy that enabled Britannia to rule the waves.

l. 11. *ignorant demagogues*: Turkish rulers suppressing the Balkan rebels.

l. 13. *triple empire*. By 1652 the Republican forces under Cromwell controlled England, Ireland, and Scotland.

27 *Ave Maria Plena Gratia*. First words in Latin of the Roman Catholic prayer 'Hail Mary full of grace'.

l. 4. *Danae*. See 'The Theatre at Argos', l. 7.

l. 5. *Semele*: a paramour of Zeus, she desired him to visit her in all his godly splendour. He did so, and she was consequently destroyed by his lightning. Their child was Dionysos.

28 *Wasted Days*. Violet Troubridge, a young artist friend, showed Wilde her picture with two scenes: on the left, a boy outside in winter looks longingly into the home of a family feasting at Christmas; on the right the same boy idles while harvesters are at work. The motto reads: 'He must hunger in frost that will not work in heate'. Shown in Mason, pp. 96–7. Wilde later adapted ll. 1–7 to describe a girl in 'Madonna Mia'.

l. 14. Cf. John 9: 4.

28 *The Grave of Shelley*. Like that of Keats, in the Protestant Cemetery at Rome. Cf. *Miscellanies*, 1–4. Shelley died by drowning.

29 *Santa Decca*: a mountain on Corfu. According to Christian tradition, on the day Christ died, a cry swept over the ocean, 'Great Pan is dead', and the oracles ceased. Cf. Gautier's poem 'Bûchers et tombeaux'.

l. 2. *olive-leaves*: the olive tree was Pallas Athena's gift to Athens.

l. 3. *Demeter's child*. Proserpine, like her mother, was honoured as a goddess of the harvest.

ll. 4–5. In Greece it was thought wise to be quiet at noon, for Pan napped then and would be angered if disturbed.

l. 7. *Hylas*: Herakles' page, who disappeared while looking for water, pulled into a stream and drowned by water nymphs enamoured of his beauty.

29 *Theoretikos*. The Contemplative: an early declaration of the ideal propounded at length in *The Critic as Artist*.

l. 5. *that voice*: Wordsworth's.

29 l. 14. Quoting Pater's *Renaissance*, 'neither for Jehovah nor for His enemies'.

30 *Amor Intellectualis*. Intellectual Love.

ll. 10–14. Browning's *Sordello* was based on the story of a thirteenth-century troubadour; *Tamburlaine the Great* is a play by Marlowe; and Dante saw the seven heavens in the *Paradiso*. 'Endymion' refers to Keats: see headnote to 'Endymion'.

30 *At Verona*. This poem echoes a description in the *Paradiso* of Dante's exile. Political intriguers in Florence exiled Dante: in Verona he found uneasy refuge with Can Grande della Scala, the 'Hound' of l. 4. Cf. *Letters*, 9.

l. 4. Cf. Matthew 15: 27.

l. 9. Job's wife encouraged him to do the same: Job 2: 9.

l. 14. A deliberate echo of the ending of the *Divine Comedy*: 'The Love that moves the sun and the other stars'. Cf. 'Apologia', l. 36.

31 *Ravenna*. Won the Newdigate Prize in Oxford for 1878. Wilde had visited Ravenna in 1877. Ravenna was a strategic harbour of the Roman Empire, became the chief residence of the Western Emperors in the fourth century, and served as the capital of Italy under the Ostrogoths. But by Wilde's visit, all the glory was in the past, and large sections of the city were deserted.

l. 17. *water-king*: kingfisher.

32 l. 49. *Proserpine, with poppy-laden head*: queen of Hades and of Sleep.

l. 60. *Gaston de Foix*: leader of the French siege of Ravenna in 1512, he was killed in the course of defeating the Spanish and Italian army sent to relieve the city. The Colonne dei Francesi was erected where he fell.

33 l. 71. *Theodoric*: king of the Ostrogoths who conquered the city in 495. He was buried in a tomb erected by his daughter.

l. 79. *great queen*: Florence; cf. l. 100.

l. 80. *Dante*: exiled from Florence, he died in Ravenna.

l. 86. *Giotto*: Florentine artist and architect: his tower (l. 91) is a Florentine landmark.

l. 89 ff. Cf. 'At Verona' headnote.

l. 102. *empty tomb*. A monument was erected for Dante in Florence, but Ravenna refused to give up his remains.

l. 105. *Beatrice*. Dante (1265–1321) early fell in love with the girl he celebrates as Beatrice in the *Vita Nuova* and the *Divine Comedy*. She died young, but inspired his poetry, and in the *Divine Comedy* met him in the earthly paradise of the *Purgatorio*, and guided him to the *Paradiso*.

34 l. 113. *Byron*. In Ravenna 1819–21. He went to join the war in Greece for independence from the Turks in 1823.

l. 114. *Anthony*: his love for Cleopatra alienated him from Rome. His supporters managed to control the port at Ravenna, but Octavian defeated the lovers at Actium.

ll. 128–33. Sites where the Greeks had fended off the Persian invasion of the fifth century BC.

35 ll. 145–50. *crowns*: see 'Roses and Rue' headnote.

l. 146. *Sapphic Mitylene*: see 'The Grave of Keats' l. 10.

l. 173. *Hylas*: see 'Santa Decca' l. 7 n.

36 l. 184. *Caesar*: Augustus made Ravenna the main naval base for the upper Adriatic.

l. 189. *deserted by the sea*. Sediment carried by the river Po silted up the estuary, and by the time of Wilde's visit Ravenna lay six miles inland.

l. 200. *Italia's royal warrior*. Victor Emmanuel II, king of united Italy, entered Rome and made it his capital in 1871.

l. 205–12. Victor Emmanuel originally ruled Genoa. He recovered Milan from Austria in 1859, became king of Naples in 1860, after the city had deposed its Bourbon ruler, Francis II, and won Venice from the Austrians in 1866. His occupation of Rome fulfilled Dante's dream of an Italy free of foreign interlopers.

37 l. 222. *ice-crowned citadels*: the Alps.

ll. 226–7. Battle-grounds on which Italian forces met defeat during the wars for the unification of Italy.

38 ll. 246–9. Obscure. Adria was the name of the town originally settled by the Thessalians, Greek traders who had crossed the Adriatic. Under the Caesars, Ravenna's navy helped to maintain the Empire's sovereignty. After the deaths of Theodoric and his daughter, Justinian, Emperor of the Eastern Empire, sent Belisarius to regain control of the Western Empire from the Ostrogoths. His success established Ravenna as the seat of Byzantine dominion in Italy. In this sense the city could have been a 'Queen of double Empires'.

ll. 270–1. *Dome . . . drear Campagna*: St Peter's rising above the marshy Campagna around Rome. Cf. 'Rome Unvisited' l. 27.

l. 273. *city of the violet crown*: Athens.

l. 275. *'myriad laughter'*. J. A. Symonds used this phrase in describing the *Prometheus Bound* of Aeschylus.

38 l. 280. *twenty summers*. Wilde was 22 when he visited Ravenna, but hedging about his age was characteristic.

39 l. 295. *lone chapel . . . marshy plain*. The church of Sta Maria in Porto Fuori lay two miles from the city on the site of the old harbour.

40 *Magdalen Walks*. Wilde was at Magdalen College, Oxford, from 1874 to 1878.

41 *The Burden of Itys. Burden*: the low under-song or accompaniment to a melody. Philomela was raped by Tereus, king of Thrace, and husband to her sister Procne. He cut out her tongue, but Philomela wove a tapestry to tell her sister, who sought revenge by killing her son Itys and serving the body to her husband. When he in turn sought revenge, Procne was changed into a nightingale, which ever mourns for the son, and Philomela into a swallow. But here Wilde follows the Latin authors, who have Philomela transformed into the nightingale rather than Procne. This poem makes a sustained comparison of the ancient world and the Oxford countryside: places are not glossed unless especially significant.

l. 6. *crystal-hearted star*: the monstrance, a glass-framed shrine, usually in the form of a sun emitting its rays to all sides, in which the consecrated Host can be publicly displayed.

ll. 9–12. *monsignores . . . Bishop* in partibus. The religious analogy continues—monsignores are senior clerics; a bishop *in partibus* is titular bishop of a non-Christian area.

l. 14. *Palæstrina*: sixteenth-century Italian composer who was choirmaster at Sta Maria Maggiore, near Rome.

42 l. 29. *Esquiline*: one of the hills of Rome.

l. 37. *Fra Giovanni*: Brother John; a general type, not a specific person.

l. 38. *bird*: the nightingale. Cf. throughout Keats's 'Ode to a Nightingale', although Keats does not use the Philomela myth.

l. 57. *Daphnis*: the legendary originator of pastoral poetry.

l. 58. *song of Linus*. Herakles killed his music teacher Linus with his own lyre. A song of mourning was sung annually at harvest from Homeric times.

43 l. 61. *Lycoris*: the name under which Cytheris, the mistress of the Roman poet Gallus, was celebrated in his poetry.

l. 63. *amaracine*: aromatic.

l. 72. *heavenly herdsman*: Apollo. Cf. l. 173.

l. 93. *Syrinx*: a nymph, pursued by Pan, who was transformed into a reed-bed to frustrate his intentions. He made his pipe from her reeds.

l. 95. *Cytheræa*: Aphrodite.

44 l. 103. *Danae*. See note to 'The Theatre at Argos', l. 7.

ll. 105–6. *Mercury . . . Dis*. Mercury guided the souls of the dead to the netherworld, where reigned Dis, a Roman name for Hades, also known to the Romans as Pluto.

l. 110. *Arachne*: for her presumption in challenging Athena to a weaving contest, she was transformed by the goddess into a spider.

l. 116. *Narcissus*: he fell in love with his own image reflected in a stream.

l. 120. *Salmacis*: a nymph of a fountain in which a young boy bathed. She embraced him and asked the gods to make them one body, and they were transformed into a hermaphrodite.

l. 126. *Oreads*: nymphs of the mountains.

l. 127. *Ariadne*: she helped Theseus slay the Minotaur, but he deserted her on the island of Naxos, where Dionysos discovered her and made her his wife.

45 l. 132. *Maeonia's bard*: the blind poet Homer, author of the *Iliad*, to the plot of which epic the next stanza refers.

l. 139. *Perseus*: the son of Jupiter and Danae who slew the Gorgon Medusa, whose hair was made of snakes, and the sight of whom turned men to stone.

l. 153. *wondrous boy*: Swinburne, author of *Atalanta in Calydon*.

l. 159. *the shepherd*: Matthew Arnold, who as 'Corydon' mourned Arthur Hugh Clough in his pastoral poem 'Thyrsis', set around Oxford but in a Greek mode.

46 l. 165. *little clan*: D. G. Rossetti, poet and painter, a founder of the Pre-Raphaelite Brotherhood, a group of artists determined to abandon the academic painting that had prevailed since Raphael, and return to Nature and the earlier purity of style of fourteenth- and fifteenth-century Tuscan fresco painters.

l. 173. *son of Leto*: Apollo, the protector of flocks and herds.

l. 175. *Bacchus*: Dionysos, god of mirth, who as one of his manifestations in Asia Minor appeared as conqueror of India.

l. 179. *Bassarid*: a male votary of Dionysos.

l. 181. *leopard skin*: the dress of Pan, a sometime companion of Dionysos.

l. 182. *Ashtaroth*: Astarte, the Syrian Aphrodite. A moon-goddess, she rides on the moon. Cf. 'Charmides', l. 538.

l. 189. *Mænad*: a female votary of Dionysos.

46 l. 197. *hornèd master*: Pan, whose satyrs are also referred to as Pans (see l. 190).

47 l. 200. *Apollo's lad*: Hyacinth. Cf. ll. 205–7, and see 'The Garden of Eros', l. 79 n.

l. 201. *Tyrian prince*: Adonis, beloved of Aphrodite. He was killed by a boar, and his body was sought by the goddess (cf. ll. 208–10). Cf. l. 582 n. of 'Charmides'.

l. 204. *virgin maid*: Artemis, goddess of the hunt, was known by the epithet 'stag-killer'.

l. 208. *Cyprian*: Aphrodite.

l. 214. *to burn one's old ships*: proverbial for cutting oneself off from the past. Roman generals burned their ships when they invaded a foreign country. Their soldiers had to push forward or die, since retreat was impossible.

l. 216. *Proteus*: a sea-god, servant of Poseidon.

l. 217. *Medea*: a witch on the island of Colchis, whose sorcery put a dragon to sleep, enabling Jason to win the Golden Fleece.

l. 220. *Proserpine*: also Persephone: daughter of Ceres, goddess of harvest, she was kidnapped from the fields of Enna by Hades, or Dis, king of the underworld. She was freed by Zeus, but because she had eaten some pomegranate seeds during her captivity, Proserpine was required to spend part of each year in the netherworld, and became Queen of Hades, death, and sleep.

l. 230. *Venus . . . Melian farm*: the Venus de Milo, a statue unearthed on the island of Melos in 1820.

l. 233. *Dawn at Florence*: sculpted by Michelangelo for the Medici Chapel, San Lorenzo, visited by Wilde in 1875 (*Letters*, 4).

48 l. 238. *riven veil*. The veil of the Temple at Jerusalem was rent in two the day Christ died.

l. 241. *Niobe*. Her boasting over her children led to their deaths at the hands of the gods. She weeps for them as the nightingale weeps for Itys.

l. 254. *Melpomene*: the muse of tragedy.

l. 266. *Endymion*. See 'Endymion' headnote.

l. 269. *Naiad*: a water nymph.

49 l. 272. *silver daughter*: Aphrodite, born of the sea, who loved the hunter Adonis.

l. 274. *Dryope*: a nymph once loved by Apollo.

l. 278. *Daphne*: in desperate escape from the attentions of Apollo, she was transformed into a laurel tree.

l. 279. *Salmacis*: see above, l. 120.

l. 282. *Antinous*: beautiful page of the emperor Hadrian, and greatly beloved by him, he drowned mysteriously in the Nile, AD 130.

l. 293. *Marsyas*: a Phrygian flute-player, who challenged Apollo to a contest of skill, but being beaten by the god was flayed alive for his presumption.

50 l. 306. *Pandion*: father of Philomela and Procne.

ll. 307–8. See headnote.

l. 320. *swinked*: toil-worn.

51 *Theocritus*. Theocritus was a founder of Greek pastoral poetry, and Wilde's poem celebrates figures and incidents mentioned in his idylls.

l. 1. Theocritus is now in the underworld. He invokes Persephone in Idyll xv, for the protection of Sicily.

l. 3. *Sicily*. His earliest idylls were composed there.

l. 5. *Amaryllis*: in Idyll iii, the mistress of the young goatherd whose gifts of love she rejects.

l. 7. *Simætha . . . Hecate*. In Idyll ii, Simætha casts a spell to draw her fickle lover back to her, calling upon the moon-goddess Hecate to help the magic. Hecate was also goddess of the cross-roads, where monthly offerings of dog's flesh were made to her.

l. 11. *Polypheme*: in Idyll xi, a cyclops who sings of his unrequited love for the nymph Galatea.

l. 14. *Daphnis*: in Idyll vi, a shepherd who challenges his friend Damoetas to a contest of song.

52 l. 16. *Lacon*: in Idyll v, Comatas and Lacon have a song competition, the winner to gain a sheep from the flock of the loser. Comatas won: here Lacon prepares to pay his debt.

52 *Endymion*. Endymion was loved by the Moon, or the chaste goddess Artemis: in one version, she cast a spell of perpetual sleep over him so that every night she could descend to embrace or admire him. Here the speaker is a shepherdess in love with Endymion. Wilde's favourite poet was Keats, author of a long poem called *Endymion*, and he referred to Keats as 'the young Endymion': in 'The Garden of Eros' he refers to himself as 'the last Endymion'.

l. 22. *Helice*: Calisto of Helice, beloved of Zeus, was transformed by a jealous Hera into a she-bear, whereupon Zeus placed her among the stars as Ursa Major.

53 *Charmides*. The plot is taken from a hint in Lucian's *Essays in*

Portraiture, where an admirer assaults Praxiteles' statue of Aphrodite. Wilde makes the assault more shocking by making the victim the virgin goddess Athena. He takes the name Charmides from Plato's dialogue where this beautiful young man discusses with an admiring Socrates temperance, or soundness of mind. Ironically, in the dialogue, because of his beauty, both men and youths stared at him as though he were a statue.

53   l. 7. *spear*: the huge statue of Athena Nike on the Acropolis.

l. 19. *fishes' juice*: the Tyrian purple dye made from molluscs.

54   ll. 33–4. Athena was protectress of the city of Athens and its environs, as well as goddess of wisdom, war, and the liberal arts.

55   ll. 65–72. Armed for battle, Athena was traditionally depicted as wearing a helmet ornamented with griffins and heads of rams, horses, and sphinxes; armed with a shield, the aegis (more accurately a cuirass) on which hung the head of the Gorgon Medusa, and grasping a spear. She was often accompanied by an owl, her sacred bird.

56   ll. 85–90. The carved figures of the Parthenon seem to come alive.

l. 96. *shepherd prince*: Paris, who had to choose the fairest of Hera, Aphrodite, or Athena. His choice of Aphrodite brought him Helen and ultimately the ruin of Troy.

57   l. 121. *Numidian javelins*. The Numidae, nomad horsemen of Berber stock, were excellent horsemen from what is now the eastern part of Algeria.

58   l. 164. *Hylas*. See 'Santa Decca', l. 7 n.

l. 170. *Dionysos*: god of mirth; the Bassarid was a votary of his.

l. 181. *neat-herd's lad*: a cattle-herder's apprentice.

60   l. 240. *Orion*: the hunter Orion was transformed into a constellation. *Mars*: the planet.

61   l. 277. *Triton-god*: a merman.

62   l. 289. *Colonos*: a hill a mile north of Athens.

l. 292. *Hymettus*: a mountain east of Athens, famous for its honey.

l. 297. *Hyacinth*. see 'The Burden of Itys', l. 200 n.

l. 301. *Dryads*: forest-nymphs, whose lives were bound up with the trees they inhabited: cf. ll. 452 ff.

l. 303. *Pan*: the god Pan's satyrs are also referred to as Pans.

l. 304. *Poseidon*: Greek god of the sea, notoriously profligate.

64   l. 358. *froward*: disposed to go counter to what is demanded or required.

l. 360. *Proserpine*: queen of the netherworld.

l. 384. *Proteus*: a sea-god who herded the seals.

65 l. 405. *lovely boy*: Eros, or Cupid.

l. 409. *the laurel*: Daphne. Cf. 'The Burden of Itys', l. 278 n.

ll. 410–13. *Boreas*: the North Wind, a violent deity who abducted youths and nymphs and even fathered horses.

l. 414. *Hermes*. Rebuked by Zeus for cleverness and deceit, Hermes was herald of the gods, and conveyed the dead to the netherworld.

66 l. 437. *Cytheræa*: Aphrodite.

67 ll. 470–1. *Amaryllis . . . Daphnis*. See notes to 'Theocritus', ll. 5, 14.

l. 478. *Paphian myrtles*: trees of Cyprus, a centre for the worship of Aphrodite.

l. 487. *Cyprian Queen*: Venus, with Adonis.

68 ll. 490–1. *moon . . . Endymion's eyes*. See headnote to 'Endymion'.

l. 498. *Xiphias*: sword-fish.

69 l. 538. *doves . . . wane*. Aphrodite is riding on the moon (cf. l. 572) which is drawn by her sacred birds.

70 l. 582. *Thammuz*: Adonis, Aphrodite's lover, who was killed by a boar. Aphrodite petitioned Zeus, and Adonis was permitted to leave the netherworld and spend part of each year with her. Thus he is alive at l. 536.

71 l. 603. *Proserpine*: queen of the netherworld: see 'The Burden of Itys', l. 220 n.

l. 606. *Charon's icy ford*. The ferryman conveyed the dead across the river Styx to Hades.

l. 607. *Acheron*: a river of the netherworld and its swampy surroundings, or hell itself.

l. 613. *Lethæan well*: the waters of forgetfulness.

72 l. 639. *Icarus*. While escaping from Crete on wings of wax and feathers, he soared too near the sun, and the wax melted. He fell into the sea and drowned.

l. 642. The poet Sappho committed suicide by throwing herself into the sea off the island of Lesbos.

ll. 652–4. Another reference to the rape of Proserpine: see 'The Burden of Itys', l. 220 n.

73 *Ballade de Marguerite*. A particularly derivative poem (from D. G. Rossetti's 'John of Tours (Old French)'): Wilde rather repudiated it in the 1890s (*Letters*, 325). The language is deliberately archaic.

l. 18. *morte*: a flourish sounded at the death of a beast in hunting.

74 *Humanitad.* The title presumably means 'Humanity', a combination of Latin and Spanish. Wilde's detailed display of old-fashioned flower names is not glossed.

75 l. 7. *Saturn's cave.* In Keats's *Hyperion*, ii, the old gods, the Titans, overthrown by the Olympians, gather together in a cave where they, and Saturn their head, bemoan their fate.

77 l. 83. *nepenthe*: a drug that induces forgetfulness of grief.

78 l. 103. *clear flame.* Cf. Wilde's master Pater, in the notorious Conclusion to *The Renaissance* (1873): 'To burn always with this hard, gem-like flame, to maintain this ecstasy, is success in life'.

l. 107. *Medea.* See 'The Burden of Itys', l. 217 n.

l. 112. *Swan's death.* According to legend, a swan which has lost its mate calls for it to the end of its days.

l. 113. *Memnon.* Cf. *The Sphinx*, ll. 133–4.

l. 117. *XAIPE*: welcome.

l. 121. *poppy-crownèd God*: Hades, lord of the netherworld.

l. 132. *brows Olympian*: Aphrodite, goddess of love.

l. 137. *Artemis*: Diana, virgin goddess of hunting.

79 l. 149. *Hers.* Athena, the virgin goddess, wears the Gorgon's head on her cuirass; cf. 'Charmides', ll. 65–72 n.

l. 151. *dainty page*: Cupid.

l. 154. *Adonis.* See 'Charmides', l. 682 n.

l. 157. *shepherd boy*: Paris. Cf. 'Charmides', l. 96 n.

l. 159. *Tenedos . . . Troy.* Cities associated with tragic love. Tenes' stepmother fell in love with him, and when he refused her advances accused him publicly of improper advances. He was set adrift in a chest by his outraged father, and eventually landed at Tenedos. Troy recalls the love of Paris and Helen.

l. 160. *Queen*: Aphrodite.

l. 163. *Athena.* See 'Charmides', ll. 33–4 n.

l. 166. *One who . . . died to show*: Byron. Cf. *Ravenna*, l. 113.

l. 167. *Marathon.* The Greek victory over the Persians in 490 BC became a symbol of free men opposing an invading despot.

l. 169. *Portico*: a public ambulatory in Athens to which the Stoic Zeno (l. 172) and his disciples resorted.

80 l. 177. *Colonos*: the burial place of Oedipus, who had saved Thebes by answering the riddle of the Sphinx.

l. 178. *Mnemosyne*: mother of the muses.

l. 180. *Athena's owl*: a symbol of wisdom.

l. 183. *Muse of Time*: Clio, the muse of historians.

l. 186. *Polymnia's scroll.* Technically, Polymnia was the muse of lyric poetry, not history. Though Aeschylus' play *The Persians* might be classed as poetry, the specific details of the Persian invasion of Greece in 480 BC recorded in ll. 186–204 are recorded in Herodotus' *History*, not Aeschylus.

l. 188. *little town*: Athens.

l. 190. *the Mede*: Xerxes, king of the Persians.

l. 192. *Artemisium . . . Thermopylæ.* The Greek fleet was stationed at Artemisium. Thermopylæ was a hot spring adjacent to a pass through which the Persians hoped to gain entry to the Grecian lowlands. They forced the pass by circling over the mountains on a narrow trail and outflanking the defenders on the other side. Leonidas, king of the Spartans, ordered a general retreat, but stayed with 300 followers to fight against overwhelming odds until they were killed to a man.

l. 202. *Eurotas*: the river on the banks of which Sparta was built.

l. 204. *Salamis.* At the straits of Salamis the Greek navy set an ambush and annihilated the Persian fleet.

l. 207. *Dial's wheel*: clock mechanism.

81 l. 213. *Helvellyn.* These hills, like the environs of Mount Rydal, were the haunts of Wordsworth.

l. 226. *Hydra*: a many-headed monster which Herakles decapitated with his sword. The 'hydra' became a popular figure for anything destructive and multifarious, such as Falsehood in the present context.

l. 229. *Ichabod.* Cf. 1 Samuel 4: 21. An Old Testament name, Ichabod means 'The glory has departed'. Hence the use of the word as an exclamation.

ll. 230–87. *son of Italy.* Giuseppe Mazzini (1805–72), the Italian revolutionary, was at once a religious mystic and anti-cleric who saw himself summoned to the 'apostolate' of liberating and unifying Italy. His writings and organizational abilities led to his election as triumvir (l. 246) of the short-lived Roman republic which was proclaimed in 1849 and snuffed out in 1850. He was buried in Genoa, not Florence: Wilde's admonitions to Florence as the keeper of his tomb are misplaced.

l. 233. *Giotto's tower*: in Florence. Cf. note to *Ravenna*, l. 86.

l. 237. *conqueror.* Mazzini, because of his political opinions, lived most of his life as an exile outside Italy. He did return in 1848, and when Pope Pius IX had abandoned Rome to the republican rebels, Mazzini entered Rome in triumph, and was shortly afterwards elected head of the republic.

81 l. 242. *old man . . . rusty keys*. A derisive reference to Pius IX, who as pope was keeper of the keys of St Peter.

82 l. 250. *Valdarno*: the valley cut by the river Arno.

l. 251. *Brunelleschi*: architect of the dome of the cathedral in Florence. *Melpomene*: the muse of tragedy.

l. 254. *the Nine*: the muses.

l. 257. *Marathon*: see above, l. 167 and note.

l. 273. *everlasting gates*: cf. Psalm 24: 7.

l. 278. *red harlotries*: the whore of Babylon in Revelation 17: 3, which Protestants have traditionally identified as the Roman Catholic Church.

ll. 279–82. 'The Aeginetans', a pediment group from a Doric temple on Aegina, was removed to Munich. The sculpture shows combatants before the walls of Troy. See Pater's 1880 essay on 'The Marbles of Aegina', reprinted in *Greek Studies*.

83 l. 287. *Niobe*. She boasted inordinately of the number of her children, whereupon the gods slew them and turned her into a stone which still shed tears.

l. 291. *graveclothes*: cf. John 20: 5–7.

l. 298. *Aspromonte*: in Calabria, where republicans attempting to march on Rome in 1862 met defeat at the hands of the Italian army.

ll. 307–8. *mighty sword . . . righteously*: possibly the sword of Goliath; in I Samuel 17, David stunned the giant with his slingshot, but, lacking a sword, took Goliath's and slew him with it.

l. 310. *voiceless tripod*. In Christian tradition, the ancient Greek oracles, which spoke from flaming tripods, were silenced for ever by the death of Christ. Cf. headnote to 'Santa Decca'.

84 l. 325. *Cromwell spared*. During the English Revolution, the Puritan army often defaced monuments and buildings.

l. 330. *new Vandals*. William Morris founded a society to protect old buildings from the ignorant and damaging 'restorations' being attempted.

l. 331. *Art*: Gothic art, by anonymous collectives of artisans.

l. 332. *Lincoln's lofty choir*: the Angel choir of Lincoln Cathedral, renowned for its complex gothic tracery.

l. 337. *Southwell's arch . . . the House*: Southwell Minster, an example of the luxuriant sculptured foliage which enjoyed a brief vogue during the thirteenth century.

l. 344. *incestuous Queen*: Cf. the plot of Shakespeare's *Hamlet*.

85 ll. 353–4. *Agnolo's | Gaunt blinded Sibyl*: the Persian Sibyl of Michelangelo, in the Sistine Chapel.

l. 355. *Titian's little maiden*: *The Presentation of the Virgin in the Temple* at Venice's Accademia. See Pater's essay 'The School of Giorgione' in *The Renaissance*.

l. 363. *Athena's shrine*: the Parthenon, with a sculptured frieze around the Temple.

86 l. 405. *live each other's lives*. A major theme of *The Soul of Man*. See also *The Ballad of Reading Gaol*, ll. 394–6.

87 l. 420. *own real hearts*. Prefiguring *Dorian Gray*.

l. 432. *Word was Man*. Cf. John 1: 1.

l. 437. *hyssop-laden rod*. During the Crucifixion, a hyssop rod dipped in vinegar was offered Christ to assuage his thirst (John 19: 29).

87 *Athanasia*. Immortality. Original title, 'The Conqueror of Time'.

l. 1. *House of Art*: the British Museum, which was increasingly filled with the results of scientific archaeology: Rossetti was inspired by artefacts he found there to 'The Burden of Nineveh', and Wilde by the Egyptian antiquities in *The Sphinx*.

88 ll. 25–6. *nightingale . . . cruel king*. See headnote to 'The Burden of Itys'.

l. 34. *Hesperos*: the Evening Star.

89 l. 43. *Cf. Psalm* 90: 4.

l. 50. *ivory gate*. In Greek legend, the ivory gate issued false dreams, the gate of horn true ones.

89 *The New Helen*. Written in honour of Lillie Langtry, famed beauty who became an actress and close friend of the Prince of Wales. Wilde paid much public tribute to her beauty, signing his *Poems* (1881) for her, 'To Helen, formerly of Troy, now of London'.

l. 4. *impassioned boy*: Paris, who abducted Helen with Aphrodite's help.

l. 12. *thy temple*: a shrine of Astarte, the Canaanite and Egyptian goddess of erotic love.

90 ll. 22–3. Sarpedôn and Memnôn were allies of the Trojans slain in the war. Cf. *The Sphinx*, ll. 133–4 n.

ll. 24–7. Hector ran from Achilles for the safety of Troy (Ilion), but was caught and killed.

l. 32. *Calypso*. She held Odysseus captive for seven years, hoping to persuade him to become her husband.

l. 41. *hollow hill*. See *The Ballad of Reading Gaol*, l. 486 n.

90 l. 43. *Erycine*: Aphrodite.

l. 45. *Her*: Mary the mother of Jesus; cf. Luke 2: 35.

91 l. 51. *lotos-leaves*. In Homer, these induced forgetfulness, even of death.

l. 62. *bird*. The swan was the sacred bird of Apollo.

l. 66. *Euphorion*. In Goethe's *Faust* Euphorion, the spirit of Romantic Poetry, was the child of Faust and Helen: cf. *Miscellanies*, 444, and Pater's 'Winckelmann' in *The Renaissance*.

l. 77. *no other god save him*: Eros. But a deliberate echo also of Exodus 20: 3.

ll. 81–3. Aphrodite sprang forth from the sea foam and made her home on the island of Cytherea.

ll. 84–6. *immortal star*. A deliberate echo of the birth of Christ. Cf. Matthew 2, Luke 2.

l. 87. *asps of Egypt*. Cleopatra killed herself with an asp's bite.

92 l. 89. *poppies*: symbols of sleep and the netherworld.

l. 92. *Tower of ivory*. Deliberate echo of the Roman Catholic Litany of the Blessed Virgin: cf. Song of Solomon 7: 4.

l. 95. *World's Desire*: Christ. See Haggai 2: 7.

92 *Panthea*. 'Panthea' was the name of an Oceanid in Shelley's *Prometheus Bound*. This poem argues from sensations back to a pantheistic vision of Nature, finding solace in the continuity of the natural world.

93 l. 30. Cf. Matthew 5: 45.

ll. 31–9. Modelled closely on Tennyson's 'The Lotos-Eaters'.

l. 46. *twelve maidens*: the Hours.

l. 47. *Endymion*. See headnote to 'Endymion'.

l. 51. *Ganymede*: a beautiful boy whom an eagle bore away from the mountains of Ida to Olympus, where he became Zeus' cupbearer.

94 l. 56. *the shepherd*: Adonis.

l. 59 *Salmacis*. See 'The Burden of Itys', l. 120 n.

l. 67. *Lethæan spring*: one of the rivers of the netherworld, to drink of which means forgetfulness.

l. 85. *ferry-man*: Charon, who conveyed the shades of the dead across the rivers of the netherworld. As his fee a bronze coin was traditionally put into the mouth of the deceased.

95 l. 90. Implicit denial of the Resurrection.

97 l. 164. *dædal-fashioned*: cunningly.

97 *Phèdre.* Original title: 'To Sarah Bernhardt'. In 1879 Bernhardt appeared in London in Racine's *Phèdre* as the heroine consumed with love for her stepson.

l. 3. *Mirandola*: an exponent of Renaissance Platonism, he spent his last years in Florence, where he was associated with the Platonic Academy. See Pater's essay 'Pico Della Mirandola' in *The Renaissance*.

l. 4. *cool olives of the Academe*: on the banks of the Cephissus, a river near Athens, once owned by Academus: here Plato taught philosophy, and so his school was called the Academy.

ll. 7–8. In Homer's *Odyssey* vi, Nausicaa and her maidens were playing with a ball near the bushes where Odysseus was sleeping, and their cries woke him.

98 *Queen Henrietta Maria.* Written to Ellen Terry, who played the queen in W. G. Wills's *Charles I*, in June 1879.

98 *Louis Napoleon.* An elegy to the son of Napoleon III, deposed ruler of France. He was killed, aged 23, in the Zulu campaign of 1879, marking the end of hopes for a Bonapartist revival in France.

l. 1. *Eagle of Austerlitz*: Napoleon Bonaparte, who earned the epithet by masterminding the great French victory at Austerlitz in 1805.

l. 5. *flaunt thy cloak of red*: i.e. threaten republican France with his claims to the throne.

l. 7. *returning legions.* An allusion to Napoleon's triumphant return to Paris after his escape from Elba.

99 *Madonna Mia.* Deliberate double meaning: either my [secular] lady, or the Blessed Virgin. An extensive revision of 'Wasted Days' (q.v.).

l. 1. *lily-girl.* Maybe, like 'The New Helen', this poem is written for Lillie Langtry.

ll. 12–14. Cf. Dante's *Paradiso*, xxi, where the poet and his Beloved have ascended to Saturn, the seventh heaven beneath the constellation Leo, and see a golden ladder reaching on above them out of sight.

99 *Roses and Rue.* See Swinburne's 'Ave atque Vale', which begins: 'Shall I strew on thee rose or rue or laurel . . . ?' The rose symbolizes love; rue, pity and remembrance.

102 *Portia.* Written to Ellen Terry, who starred in *The Merchant of Venice* in London from November 1879.

102 *Apologia.* Self-defence and justification. Cf. Swinburne's poem of the same title, and J. H. Newman's *Apologia pro Vita Sua*.

l. 8. Cf. Mark 9: 48.

103 l. 26. *daisy*: sacred to Apollo, the Sun God.

l. 36 Cf. the last line of Dante's *Paradiso*: 'The Love that moves the sun and the other stars'.

103 *Quia Multum Amavi*: Because I have loved much. Swinburne published his 'Quia Multum Amavit' in 1871. Cf. also Luke 7: 47.

104 *Silentium Amoris*. The Silence of Love.

105 Her Voice. Apparently this poem and the next were once one poem entitled 'A Farewell'.

106 My Voice.

ll. 9–10. Echo of Pater's famous account of the *Mona Lisa*.

106 Γλυκύπικρος ἔρως. Bittersweet Love.

107 l. 6. *Bice*: Beatrice, who, accompanied by a procession of elders and angels, first greets Dante in the earthly paradise of *Purgatorio*, xxx–xxxiii. See *Ravenna*, l. 105 n.

ll. 7–8. Dante saw the rising and setting of the sun while climbing the seven circles of Purgatory. The heavens opened for him in the *Paradiso*.

108 *The Garden of Eros*.

ll. 19–20. *Persephone . . . Dis*. See 'The Burden of Itys', l. 220 n.

109 l. 26. *Hylas*. See 'Santa Decca', l. 7 n.

110 l. 53. *Cytheræa's lips*. Adonis was a lover of Cytheræa, or Venus; see 'Charmides', l. 582 n. His flower, the anemone, is called 'the Tyrian King' in l. 56.

111 l. 72. *vail*: bow in homage.

l. 78. *Artemis*. The hunter Actaeon was transformed into a stag and killed by his own hounds because he had surprised the virgin goddess Artemis disrobing for her bath.

l. 79. *jacinth*: a flower which sprang from the blood of Hyacinth, beloved of Apollo, who was accidentally killed by a discus that Apollo threw. The boy's blood nourished the flowers named after him, and the petals are flecked with the words 'woe, woe'.

ll. 81–3. Cf. title note to 'The Burden of Itys'.

l. 84. Daphne (the laurel) remembers Apollo's pursuit.

l. 85. *Proserpina*. See 'The Burden of Itys', l. 220 n.

l. 87. *Helena*: Helen of Troy.

l. 92. *Cynthia*: the moon-goddess. For her love of Endymion, see the introductory note to 'Endymion'.

l. 98. *Her face*: Athena's. The Parthenon, her shrine, suffered extensive damage in the wars that ravaged Athens. Patron goddess of artists and craftsmen.

112 l. 103. *Spirit of Beauty*. See Shelley's 'Hymn to Intellectual Beauty', which Wilde deliberately echoes here.

l. 121. *boy*. Keats, whose death was memorialized in Shelley's *Adonais* (l. 126), is buried in Rome.

l. 128. *silver voice*: Shelley's. He was drowned. In his *Prometheus Unbound*, Panthea was a daughter of Oceanus.

l. 133. *fiery heart*: Swinburne, whose republican sympathies stirred controversy with the publication of *Songs before Sunrise* (1871), which celebrated the revolt of Italy against Austrian rule.

113 l. 137. *Hesperus*: the Evening Star.

ll. 139–50. Swinburne's *Atalanta in Calydon* dramatized a boar hunt in which the warrior-maid Atalanta took part. His 'Laus Veneris' was an embroidering of the Tannhäuser legend, for which see *The Ballad of Reading Gaol*, l. 486 n. His 'Hymn to Proserpine' celebrated the glories of paganism, influencing a generation weary of Christianity.

l. 150. *new Sign*: the Cross.

l. 157. *Morris*. *The Earthly Paradise* (1868–70) was set in Chaucer's time and employed archaisms reminiscent of Spenser. The work retold tales from Greek mythology as well as from the saga literature of the North.

ll. 163–6. Named are characters from Morris's retelling of the Icelandic stories in *Grettir the Strong* (1869), and *The Story of Sigurd the Volsung and the Fall of the Nibelungs* (1876). In the last work, Brynhild's betrothed, Sigurd, was fed a potion that made him forget her.

114 l. 200. *Dante . . . Gabriel*: Dante Gabriel Rossetti, Pre-Raphaelite painter and poet.

115 l. 202. *He*: Edward Burne-Jones, who painted *The Beguiling of Merlin* (1877) and *The Golden Stair* (1880).

l. 209. *Adon*: Adonis, slain by a boar.

l. 223. *Actæons*. See note to l. 78.

l. 227. *Endymion*. See headnote to 'Endymion'.

l. 234. *Age of Clay*. There are four ages in the histories of civilizations: Golden, Silver, Iron, and Clay, in order of increasing corruption.

116 l. 237. *Titans*: the offspring of Uranus and Earth, the Titans in turn gave birth to the Olympians, by whom they were deposed.

l. 248. *Hecate's boat*: the moon.

117 *Ave Imperatrix*. Hail to the Empress. Russian expansion in the nine-

teenth century was regarded as the greatest threat to British interests. From 1878 to 1880 Britain fought a war in Afghanistan, because its ruler had rejected British overtures and accepted a Russian mission to Cabool (Kabul). In late July 1880 an Afghan army routed the British force defending Kandahar and laid siege to the city. Troops were dispatched from Cabool to relieve Kandahar, but when Wilde published his poem, in August 1880, Britain was still in suspense over its fate.

117 l. 13. *leopards*: heraldic term for lions, traditional emblem of Great Britain.

l. 14. *Russian*: opponent of British troops in the Crimean War, 1854–6.

l. 17. *sea-lion*. See note to 'To Milton', l. 10. Disraeli had sent the Royal Navy to the Dardanelles in 1878 to force a Russian peace with Turkey.

118 l. 22. *Pathan's reedy fen*: the Pathans inhabited the lowlands around Kandahar.

l. 29. *Marri*: tribesman of the Yusufzai, who inhabited the mountains near Cabool and the Khyber Pass.

l. 37. *Himalayan height*. In Wilde's day the Hindu Kush were considered an offshoot of the Himalayas.

l. 40. *wingèd dogs of Victory*. In the Roman Empire, Britain was renowned for the quality of its hunting dogs, and the Imperial soldiers worshipped figures of the winged Victory; Wilde here combines these associations.

119 l. 77. *Delhi*: centre of the Indian Mutiny of 1857. The city was retaken by the British with heavy casualties.

l. 78. *Afghan*. During the first Afghan war of 1838–42, a British garrison at Cabool had been annihilated after it had agreed to evacuate the city.

l. 79. *Ganges*. Kampur on the Ganges was the site of a notorious massacre of British troops and dependants during the Indian Mutiny.

l. 81. *Russian waters*. Combined land–sea forces suffered severely at the siege of Sebastopol during the Crimean War.

l. 83. *portals to the East*. The eastern Mediterranean, the Aegean, and the Black Sea straits all provided access to various parts of the Ottoman Empire. The British navy saw action in these waters at various times.

121 ll. 119–20. Build-up of imagery of England as The Crucified.

ll. 123–4. The Empire is 'resurrected' as a Republic.

121 *Pan*. For Pan and his passing, see headnote to 'Santa Decca'.

l. 13. *Helicé*. See 'Endymion', l. 22 n.

122 l. 32. *sea-lion*. See note to 'To Milton', l. 10.

Sen Artysty; or, The Artist's Dream. The Polish actress Helena Mod-jeska made her London début in May 1880. No Polish original has been traced.

123 l. 31. *gorgeous East*. Unlikely: West? Probably Wilde was misled by his half memory of Wordsworth's 'On the Extinction of the Venetian Republic': 'Once did she hold the gorgeous east in fee, | And was the safeguard of the west'.

l. 33. *One*. In Keats's 'The Fall of Hyperion', which Wilde is in a way replying to, the guide was Moneta, mother of the muses. Here she is Glory (ll. 41, 62), whose favour the artist pleads.

124 l. 51. *shooting arrows at the sun*: proverbial act of futility. Herakles, once angered by the heat of the day, shot arrows at the sun in an attempt to extinguish it.

l. 78. *Sirian star*: the Dog Star.

125 *Libertatis Sacra Fames*: the sacred hunger for liberty. Contemporary readers would have understood the sonnet as a criticism of the Nihilists, Russian revolutionaries who had resorted to terrorism in protesting against Czar Alexander II. This state of affairs was also the subject of Wilde's first, unsuccessful, play *Vera*.

126 *Sonnet to Liberty*.

l. 9. *discreet*: separate.

l. 14. Reference to Arnold's poem 'To a Republican Friend, 1848', which begins, 'God knows it, I am with you'.

126 *Tædium Vitæ*. Weariness of Life.

127 *Fabien dei Franchi*. Henry Irving played the twin brothers Fabien and Lucien dei Franchi in a revival of *The Corsican Brothers*, a Dion Boucicault adaptation of a novel by the elder Dumas in 1880–1. In the melodrama, Lucien is killed by his rival-in-love, Chateau Renaud. The apparition of the dead brother appears to Fabien in a famous trap-door scene where the ghost apparently materializes out of the ground. Fabien seeks revenge, killing Chateau Renaud in a duel in the last act. Irving did a series of Shakespearean revivals, playing Richard III (l. 13) in 1877. But he did not play Romeo (l. 11) until 1882, or Lear (l. 9) until 1892.

127 *Serenade*. Paris is waiting for Helen, to carry her off to Troy.

128 *Camma*. Written to Ellen Terry, who played the part of Camma, a

priestess of Artemis, in Tennyson's *The Cup* in 1881. Miss Terry never did play Cleopatra (l. 10).

129 *Impression du Matin.* Impression of the Morning. The French influence of Gautier, to Wilde 'most fascinating of modern poets', becomes evident here and later. Gautier's *Émaux et Camées* emphasized objective description free from emotional asides and didactic commentary. The connection to French Impressionist painting is also evident.

ll. 1–2. References to paintings by James McNeill Whistler, another disciple of Gautier, who famously sued Ruskin for a scornful review. 'Nocturne in Blue and Gold' and 'Harmony in Grey—Chelsea in Ice' are both Whistler paintings. Wilde's friendship with Whistler early turned sour, as the painter demanded total discipleship.

130 *In the Gold Room: A Harmony.* Reminiscent of Whistler, whose famous Peacock Room was often referred to as a 'harmony in blue and gold': see 'Impression du Matin', ll. 1–2 n.

131 *La Fuite de la Lune.* The Flight of the Moon.

131 *Impression: Le Réveillon.* In painting, 'réveillon' refers to a strong light-effect against a sombre background: a highlight.

132 *Hélas.* Alas. Placed as the introductory sonnet to *Poems*, evidently meant as Wilde's credo.

l. 2. *stringed lute.* Favourite Romantic image of the Aeolian harp, hung up and played by the wind.

l. 7. *virelay:* an old French lyric form.

ll. 12–14. In 1 Samuel 14, Saul forbade the Israelites to eat, upon pain of death, until the Philistines were defeated. His son Jonathan had tasted a honeycomb while leading his army to victory, and later confessed: 'I did but taste a little honey with the end of the rod that was in mine hand, and, lo, I must die'. Pater had quoted this verse in the 'Winckelmann' essay in his influential *The Renaissance*.

132 *Impressions: I. Le Jardin.* The Garden.

133 *La Mer.* The Sea.

133 *Le Jardin des Tuileries.* The Tuileries Gardens were the most popular promenade in Paris, especially favoured by nursemaids and their charges.

134 l. 12. *Triton:* a minor sea-god cast in the shape of a merman.

ll. 19–20. Cf. Wilde's short story 'The Selfish Giant'.

134 *The Harlot's House.* The resonance of the title is increased by reference to ch. 2 of the Book of Joshua. The poem contains deliberate echoes of Edgar Allan Poe's verses 'The Haunted Palace' from *The*

Fall of the House of Usher, plus the medieval tradition of the dance of death, or *danse macabre*, an ominous dance of the living with the dead, which had been notably used by Baudelaire and by Gautier.

l. 6. '*Treues Liebes Herz*' of *Strauss*: 'The Heart of True Love', a waltz by Viennese composer Johann Strauss (1825–99).

136 *Fantaisies Décoratives: I. Le Panneau* (The Panel), and *II. Les Ballons* (The Balloons). Wilde suggests appropriate illustrations for these, *Letters*, 206, and they were provided by John Bernard Partridge.

138 *Under the Balcony*. Probably inspired by the balcony scene in *Romeo and Juliet*, II. ii, with parallel images.

139 *Sonnet on the Sale by Auction of Keats' Love Letters*. See *More Letters*, 89–91.

l. 1. *Endymion*: Wilde often referred to Keats by the name of this poem. Cf. 'Endymion' headnote.

140 *The New Remorse*.

ll. 10–11. Deliberate echo of Isaiah 63: 1.

140 *Canzonet*. A short cheerful or lively song.

141 l. 18. *Hyacinth*. See 'The Garden of Eros', l. 79 n.

l. 19. *Pan*. See 'Santa Decca' headnote.

l. 25. *Hylas*. See 'Santa Decca', l. 7 n.

l. 30. *Dryads*: tree-nymphs.

141 *With a Copy of 'A House of Pomegranates'*. Inscribed in fact in a copy of *The Happy Prince* given to Justin McCarthy, who had published a poem called 'The Gold Girl' in his *Serapion and Other Poems* (1883).

141 *Symphony in Yellow*.

l. 1. *bridge*: Blackfriars.

142 l. 10. *Temple*: one of the Inns of Court on the Thames Embankment.

142 *In the Forest*. Like 'Fantaisies Décoratives' (above, p. 136), this was illustrated by John Bernard Partridge.

142 *The Sphinx*. The poem was begun when Wilde was at Oxford, and almost completed in Paris in 1883, but at least 14 lines were added after the final draft in the year before publication in 1894. Wilde appears to be influenced by Rossetti's poem 'The Burden of Nineveh', which was inspired by the arrival at the British Museum of a huge 'mitred minotaur', a god of Nineveh, and by his own experience of the Egyptian collections there. Otherwise, French literary influence predominates, including Baudelaire, Flaubert, Gautier, and Roll-

inat. He searches out unusual rhymes, borrowing from Flaubert terms like mandragores, oreichalch, tragelaphos. The notes will not attempt to identify all the semi-precious stones, or to draw attention to the contrast of changing textures throughout. Some phrases defy explanation, because they evolved accidentally in composition. For more detail on all these matters, see I. Murray, 'Some Problems of Editing Wilde's Poem *The Sphinx*', *Durham University Journal*, 82/1 (1990), 73–9.

143   l. 12. *half woman and half animal.* The Egyptian sphinx was generally male, while the Greek sphinx was female; Wilde deliberately confuses the traditions: his sphinx is female.

l. 18. *twenty summers.* Cf. *Ravenna*, ll. 279–81.

l. 20. *Basilisk*: fabulous reptile with lethal breath and/or evil eye, hatched by a serpent from a cock's egg! *Hippogriff*: griffin with the body of a horse.

l. 21. *Isis . . . Osiris.* Isis was the Egyptian Goddess of divine motherhood with posthumous child Horus brought up to avenge his father, Osiris, both brother and husband of Isis, killed and dismembered by his brother Seth. Thereafter Osiris was symbol of life and rebirth and lord of the dead.

l. 22. *Egyptian . . . Antony.* Cleopatra, melted her 'union', a large pearl, in wine and drank it, to show her love for Antony. In another story, she caught Antony cheating at fishing, so had a ready-salted fish attached to his line under water.

144   l. 25. *the Cyprian . . . Adon.* Venus, much worshipped in Cyprus, loved Adonis, a beautiful youth who was killed by a boar. *Catafalque*: coffin-stand.

l. 26. *Amenalk*: a form of Ammon or Amun. *Heliopolis*: a town situated not far from the head of the Delta, a highly important religious centre from very early times.

l. 27. *Thoth*: the Egyptian Hermes. *Io*: A Greek mythological priestess, beloved of Zeus; changed into a heifer to avoid Hera's pursuing champions.

l. 31. *Jewish maid . . . Holy Child.* Reference to the flight of the Holy Family into Egypt under divine guidance to escape Herod's Massacre of the Innocents (Matthew 2: 13). *Repose on the Flight into Egypt*, a painting by Luc Olivier Merson in 1879, showed Virgin and Child resting between the paws of the Sphinx.

l. 34. *Adrian . . . Antinous.* See 'The Burden of Itys', l. 282 n.

l. 37. *labyrinth . . . twy-formed Bull.* The Cretan labyrinth was said to have been designed by Daedalus for King Minos of Crete, to hide the

Minotaur, a monster with the body of a man and the head of a bull. *twy-formed*: formed of two incongruous parts.

l. 39. *scarlet Ibis*: sacred bird of ancient Egypt, the manifestation of the god Thoth. For Egyptians its white plumage symbolized the sun, and its black plumage the moon: *Britannica* notes it is a popular error, especially among painters, that the scarlet ibis (found in tropical and subtropical America) was the sacred ibis of the Eygptians.

l. 40. *moaning mandragores*: the narcotic plant mandrake, the root of which was fabled to utter a deadly shriek when plucked from the ground.

l. 41. *Crocodile*. Most Egyptian gods took the shape of some animal, which was regarded as sacred. Egyptians bred and pampered one particular member of the sacred species.

145 l. 48. *Gryphon*: a fabulous animal usually represented as having the head and wings of an eagle and the body and hindquarters of a lion.

l. 51. *Lycian tomb . . . Chimaera*: the Chimera was a fabulous monster, born in Lycia and killed by Bellerophon. Wilde writes admiringly of Flaubert's dialogue of Sphinx and Chimera.

l. 54. *Nereid*: sea-nymph.

l. 56. *Leviathan or Behemoth*: the crocodile and the hippopotamus from the Book of Job.

l. 60. *glyph*: architectural term for an ornamental groove or channel, usually vertical.

l. 61. *bar*: a bank across the mouth of a river or harbour which obstructs navigation.

l. 62. *Lúpanar*: brothel.

l. 64. *Tragelaphos*: a fabulous beast, compounded of a goat and a stag.

146 ll. 65–6. *the God of Flies who plagued the Hebrews*. The God of Flies is Baal, or Beelzebub, but it is the God of the Old Testament who sends plagues of flies, not on the Hebrews but their persecutors the Egyptians, in Exodus (8: 21–31). Wilde, typically carelessly, misremembers this, when he makes a late change: an earlier version of the line has 'that pale God with almond eyes and almond body': in the same draft he had Pasht in the next line wrongly as male: she is an Egyptian goddess in the form of a cat.

l. 67. *the Tyrian*: Adonis, see l. 25 above.

l. 68. *Ashtaroth*: a general name for all Syrian goddesses. The god of the Assyrian is the god Assur, represented with falcon head and wings.

l. 69. *talc*: a name formerly applied to various transparent, translucent, or shining minerals.

l. 70. *oreichalch*: a kind of yellow copper ore.

l. 71. *Apis*: bull-headed god.

l. 72. *nenuphar*: water-lily.

l. 74. *Ammon*: Ammon or Amun, king of the gods, also a god of fertility, said to be the procreator of the pharaohs.

l. 75. *river-horses*: hippopotami.

l. 78. *strode across the waters*: this makes Ammon reminiscent of Christ, as does the description of funeral rites below, ll. 126–8.

l. 82. *secret name*: if the secret name of a god became known, his magic powers were lessened.

147 l. 89. *cubit*: an ancient measure of length derived from the length of the forearm; usually 18–22 inches.

l. 91 *must*: new wine or juice of the grape either unfermented or before fermentation is complete. Figuratively, anything fresh or new.

l. 92. *insapphirine*: apparently a Wilde coinage, on the model of Shakespeare's use of 'incarnadine' in *Macbeth* (II. ii. 62), meaning 'could (not) make more blue'.

l. 98. *Colchian witch*: Medea; cf. 'The Burden of Itys', l. 217 n.

l. 99. *galiot*: a small galley or boat. *Corybants*: priests of the Phrygian worship of Cybele: with both words clearly chosen for sound rather than meaning, the line makes intriguing nonsense!

148 l. 110. *rose-marble monolith*. Wilde's poem is influenced by the British Museum's outstanding collection of Egyptian antiquities. In particular, a colossal head in red granite, along with its one attendant arm, now attributed to Amenophos III, seem to inspire this line, and l. 116.

l. 114. *peristyle*: a row of columns.

ll. 116–28. *giant granite hand still clenched in impotent despair*. Forces a memory of Shelley's Ozymandias, before moving into an echo of Isis' collecting the 14 pieces of the murdered Osiris and putting them together, and into a subdued memory of the death and anointing of Christ. This is underlined by the repetition in ll. 129 and 130 that 'Only one God' has died.

l. 119. *burnous*: a mantle or cloak with a hood extensively worn by Arabs and Moors.

l. 120. *Titan thews*: gigantic muscular development; *paladin*: knightly hero, renowned champion.

149 l. 131. *the hundred-cubit gate*. See also 'the Theban gate' (l. 146); the Egyptian city of Thebes was called 'the Hundred-Gated'.

l. 132. *Dog-faced Anubis*: god of the dead, with the head of a dog or jackal.

ll. 133–4. *Memnon*: an Ethiopian prince slain by Achilles in the Trojan War. There was a black statue of him at Thebes which, being struck with the rays of the morning sun, gave out musical sounds.

151 l. 159. *grey gilt-dialled towers*. Evoking Oxford with its 'dreaming spires' as site for the 'student's cell' (l. 162).

l. 161. *snake-tressed Fury*. In Dante's journey through Hell the Furies threaten him with the snake-haired Gorgon Medusa, the sight of whom turned the beholder to stone.

l. 162. *poppy-drowsy Queen*: Proserpine; see 'The Burden of Itys', l. 220 n.

l. 166. *Abana and Pharphar*: Naaman the Syrian leper, told to wash in the Jordan for a cure, at first preferred these, his own sacred rivers running through Damascus. See 2 Kings 5.

l. 170. *Atys*: or Attis; a Phrygian shepherd, beloved of Cybele, who promised her he would live in celibacy: after breaking his vow he castrated himself and died.

ll. 171–2. *on his oar*: the river Styx was one of the five rivers of Hell: the ferryman Charon ferried the spirits of the dead across, and received an obol coin as fee, which was placed in the mouth of the corpse.

l. 174. *in vain*. This phrase seems to contradict any conviction or hope otherwise found in this return to a Christian ambience at the end of the poem.

152 *The Ballad of Reading Gaol*. Wilde was moved from Wandsworth to HM Prison, Reading, called by him in the poem Reading Gaol, on 23 November 1895, and served the rest of his sentence there. While he was there, a judicial hanging was carried out, the first in the prison for eighteen years, and this inspired the poem. Charles Thomas Wooldridge, who had been a trooper in the Royal Horse Guards, was sentenced to death for the premeditated murder of his wife. The sentence was carried out on 7 July 1896 at Reading Gaol. Wilde was released on 18 May 1897, and wrote the poem in the next six months. Early editions omitted the author's name: Wilde used his prison cell number as a pen name: 'C. 3. 3.' *Letters* and *More Letters* contain a wealth of further information about the composition of the poem.

l. 1. *scarlet coat*. Poetic licence; the Royal Horse Guards uniform was dark blue with red trimmings.

152 l. 7. *Trial Men*: remand prisoners, awaiting trial.

153 ll. 37 ff. Indebted to the Young Ireland poet Denis Florence McCarthy, in his short poem, 'A New Year's Song', which is similarly balanced, and includes such lines as 'The strong man with his sinewy hand, | The weak man with his prayer', and 'The coward slave is never freed, | The brave alone are free!'

l. 41. *with a kiss*: Judas.

154 l. 61. *silent men*. A prisoner in the condemned cell was kept under continuous observation.

l. 83. *leathern thongs*. The prisoner to be executed was bound at wrists, elbows, and knees.

155 l. 96 *Caiaphas*. Caiaphas was high priest in the year Christ was crucified, and condemned him (Matthew 26: 65). The priests paid Judas to betray Christ with a kiss, and Caiaphas declared: 'it is expedient for us, that one man should die for the people' (John 11: 50).

l. 116. *peek*: usually 'peak' or pine: droop in health or spirits.

156 l. 138. *bears its fruit*. Before the modern gallows, criminals were hanged from trees, usually oak or elm, from which the leaves had been shorn. Wilde's image also incorporates the tradition that if a tree's roots were bitten by an adder, this would destroy its leaves and fruit for a season.

157 l. 167. *holy night*. Wilde here recalls and overturns a famous line from Longfellow's *The Theologian's Tale*, 1874: 'Ships that pass in the night, and speak with each other in passing'.

l. 173. *iron gin*: trap or snare.

l. 217. *tarry rope*. 'Picking oakum' was a traditional employment for prisoners, unpicking old rope for caulking ships' seams.

159 l. 223. *the stones*: sewing mailbags and breaking stones, more accepted tasks for prisoners.

l. 224. *the dusty drill*: a narrow iron drum on legs with a long handle which scooped up and dropped cups of sand; known as 'the crank', it was particularly pointless work.

l. 226. *the mill*: the treadmill, often used as a punishment.

l. 237. *for blood*. Cf. Genesis 4: 10.

l. 246. *numbered tomb*. Prisoners were kept in solitary confinement in numbered cells: Wilde's cell at Reading was C. 3. 3, the third cell on the third floor of Block C.

160 l. 280. *plumes*: ornaments of black feathers used at funerals.

l. 281. *a sponge*: shortly before his death on the cross, Jesus was offered a sponge full of vinegar.

161 l. 283. *cock crew*: in old ballads, the conventional signal for the dead to return: see e.g. 'Sweet William's Ghost'. Also of course reminiscent of Peter's denial of Christ: see Matthew 26.

ll. 289–324. *glided fast*. Wilde draws on the medieval tradition of the dance of death, or *danse macabre* here, as it had been reshaped by Baudelaire and Gautier; see 'The Harlot's House', headnote.

l. 291. *rigadoon*: lively dance for two persons.

l. 295. *mop and mow*: grimaces.

l. 313. *antics*: archaic: mountebanks or clowns.

l. 315. *gyves*: shackles.

162 l. 321. *demirep*: a woman of doubtful reputation.

l. 336. *seneschal*: steward.

l. 345. *mighty wing*: Wilde here exploits a powerful metaphor from John Bright that he had frequently used in *Salome*. Speaking in the House of Commons about the Crimean War, Bright said: 'The angel of death has been abroad throughout the land; you may almost hear the beating of his wings'.

163 l. 367. *of eight*: the hour for weekday hangings.

l. 371. *running noose*. To ensure a strong jolt and a quick death as the rope tightened, the rope ran through a metal eyelet to avoid any friction.

l. 374. *the sign*: the tolling of the bell of St Lawrence's Church, Reading, which began a quarter of an hour before the execution and continued for some time afterwards.

164 l. 392. *bitter cry*. See Genesis 27: 34.

l. 393. *bloody sweats*. See Luke's account of Christ's agony in the garden, 22: 44.

166 l. 450. *quicklime*: intended to decompose a dead body quickly.

167 l. 486. *Pope's sight*. In medieval legend, pagan erotic pleasures were still available within the hollow hill of the Venusberg. Tannhäuser, a knight who loved Venus, risked damnation, but when he asked the pope for absolution, he refused until his dry staff burst in bud. A few days later, this happened, but Tannhäuser had disappeared.

l. 490. Cf. *Hamlet*, v. i. 188–90.

168 l. 530. *bourne*. Cf. *Hamlet*, III. i. 79–80.

l. 546. *evil fan*. See Matthew 3: 12: 'Whose fan is in his hand, and he will thoroughly purge his floor, and gather his wheat into the garner; but he will burn up the chaff with unquenchable fire'.

169   l. 565. *frightened child.* See the *Daily Chronicle* of 27 May 1897 in *The Soul of Man and Prison Writings*, 159–68.

170   l. 580. *chalk and lime.* Adulteration of bread with chalk and lime was still common.

l. 612. *costliest nard.* See Mark 14: 3.

171   l. 622. *to Paradise.* See Luke 23: 43.

l. 624. *not despise.* See Psalm 51: 17.

l. 625. the Law: the sentencing judge.

l. 635. *of Cain.* With the death of his brother Abel, Cain became the first murderer. But God set a mark on Cain that forbade anyone to kill him (Genesis 4: 1–16).

l. 636. *snow-white seal.* See 2 Corinthians 1: 22; also Isaiah 1: 18.

Further Reading

Wilde's poetry has received much less critical attention than his other work, but the following all have some bearing.

Beckson, Karl (ed.), *Oscar Wilde: The Critical Heritage* (London, 1970).

Buckler, William E., 'Oscar Wilde's *chant de cygne: The Ballad of Reading Gaol* in Contextual Perspective', *Victorian Poetry*, 28/3–4 (1990), 33–41.

Buckley, Jerome H., 'Echo and Artifice: The Poetry of Oscar Wilde', *Victorian Poetry*, 28/3–4 (1990), 19–31.

Ellmann, Richard, *Oscar Wilde* (London, 1987).

Fehr, Bernhard, 'Studien zu Oscar Wildes Gedichten', in *Palaestra*, 100 (Berlin, 1918).

Fong, Bobby, 'The Poetry of Oscar Wilde: A Critical Edition', Ph.D. thesis (University of California, Los Angeles, 1978).

Gardner, Averil, 'Literary Petty Larceny: Plagiarism in Oscar Wilde's Early Poetry', *English Studies in Canada*, 8/1 (1982), 49–61.

Hart-Davis, Rupert (ed.), *The Letters of Oscar Wilde* (London, 1962).

—— *More Letters of Oscar Wilde* (London, 1985).

Heaney, Seamus, 'Speranza in Reading: On *The Ballad of Reading Gaol*', in *The Redress of Poetry* (1995), 83–102.

Hönnighausen, Lothar, *The Symbolist Tradition in English Literature: A Study of Pre-Raphaelitism and 'Fin de Siècle'* (Cambridge, 1988).

Kohl, Norbert, *Oscar Wilde: The Works of a Conformist Rebel* (Cambridge, 1989).

Mason, Stuart, *Bibliography of Oscar Wilde* (London, 1914).

Mikhail, E. H., *Oscar Wilde: An Annotated Bibliography of Criticism* (London, 1978).

Murray, Isobel, 'Some Problems of Editing Wilde's Poem *The Sphinx*', *Durham University Journal*, 82/1 (1990), 73–9.

Ransome, Arthur, *Oscar Wilde* (London, 1913).

Roditi, Edouard, *Oscar Wilde* (Norfolk, Conn. 1947).

Ross, Robert (ed.), *The Poems of Oscar Wilde* (London, 1908).

Shewan, Rodney, *Oscar Wilde: Art and Egotism* (London, 1977).

Small, Ian, *Oscar Wilde Revalued: An Essay on New Materials & Methods of Research* (Greensboro, NC, 1993).

Thomas, J. D., 'Oscar Wilde's Prose and Poetry', *Rice Institute Pamphlet*, 42 (1954), 32–52.

Index of Titles and First Lines

A fair slim boy not made for this world's pain   28
A lily-girl, not made for this world's pain   99
A ring of gold and a milk-white dove   8
A white mist drifts across the shrouds   133
A year ago I breathed the Italian air   31
Against these turbid turquoise skies   137
Αἲλινον, αἲλινον εἰπέ, τὸ δ' εὖ νικάτω   10
Albeit nurtured in democracy   125
Amor Intellectualis   30
An omnibus across the bridge   141
Apologia   102
As oftentimes the too resplendent sun   104
As one who poring on a Grecian urn   128
At Verona   30
Athanasia   87
Ave Imperatrix   117
Ave Maria Plena Gratia   27

Ballad of Reading Gaol, The   152
Ballade de Marguerite   73
Burden of Itys, The   41
By the Arno   4

Camma   128
Canzonet   140
Chanson   8
Charmides   53
Chorus of Cloud-Maidens   1
Christ, dost thou live indeed? or are thy bones   23
Cloud-maidens that float on for ever   1
Come down, O Christ, and help me! reach thy hand   26

Dear Heart I think the young impassioned priest   103
Dole of the King's Daughter, The   9

E Tenebris   26
Eagle of Austerlitz! where were thy wings   98
Easter Day   24
Endymion   52

Fabien dei Franchi   127
Fantaisies Décoratives: I. Le Panneau   136
Fantaisies Décoratives: II. Les Ballons   137
Fragment from the Agamemnon of Aeschylos, A   17
From Spring Days to Winter   2

Garden of Eros, The 108
Γλυκύπικρος ἔρως 106
Go, little book 141
Grave of Keats, The 23
Grave of Shelley, The 28

Harlot's House, The 134
He did not wear his scarlet coat 152
He was a Grecian lad, who coming home 53
Hélas! 132
Her ivory hands on the ivory keys 130
Her Voice 105
How steep the stairs within Kings' houses are 30
How vain and dull this common world must seem 97
Humanitad 74

I am weary of lying within the chase 73
I can write no stately proem 139
I have no store 140
I marvel not Bassanio was so bold 102
I reached the Alps: the soul within me burned 20
I remember we used to meet 99
I stood by the unvintageable sea 25
I too have had my dreams: ay, known indeed 122
I wandered through Scoglietto's far retreat 21
Impression de Voyage 21
Impression du Matin 129
Impression: Le Reveillon 131
Impressions: I. Le Jardin 132
Impressions: I. Les Silhouettes 130
Impressions: II. La Fuite de la Lune 131
Impressions: II. La Mer 133
In a dim corner of my room for longer than my fancy thinks 142
In the Forest 142
In the glad spring when leaves were green 2
In the Gold Room: A Harmony 130
In the lone tent, waiting for victory 98
Is it thy will that I should wax and wane 102
It is full summer now, the heart of June 108
It is full Winter now: the trees are bare 74
Italia 25
Italia! thou art fallen, though with sheen 25

La Bella Donna Della Mia Mente 7
Le Jardin des Tuileries 133
Libertatis Sacra Fames 125
Like burnt-out torches by a sick man's bed 28
Lotus Leaves 14
Louis Napoleon 98

Madonna Mia   99
Magdalen Walks   40
Milton! I think thy spirit hath passed away   27
My limbs are wasted with a flame   7
My Voice   106

Nay, let us walk from fire unto fire   92
Nay, Lord, not thus! white lilies in the spring   24
Nettles and poppy mar each rock-hewn seat   22
New Helen, The   89
New Remorse, The   140
Not that I love thy children, whose dull eyes   126

O beautiful star with the crimson mouth!   138
O fair wind blowing from the sea!   11
O Goat-foot God of Arcady!   121
O Singer of Persephone!   51
O well for him who lives at ease   10
Oft have we trod the vales of Castaly   30
Out of the mid-wood's twilight   142

Pan: Double Villanelle   121
Panthea   92
Phèdre   97
Portia   102

Quantum Mutata   26
Queen Henrietta Maria   98
Quia Multum Amavi   103

Ravenna   31
Requiescat   3
Rid of the world's injustice, and his pain   23
Rome Unvisited   5
Rome! what a scroll of History thine has been   22
Roses and Rue   99

San Miniato   4
Santa Decca   29
See, I have climbed the mountain side   4
Sen Artysty; or, The Artist's Dream   122
Serenade   127
Set in this stormy Northern sea   117
Seven stars in the still water   9
Silentium Amoris   104
Sonnet on Approaching Italy   20
Sonnet on Hearing the Dies Iræ Sung in the Sistine Chapel   24
Sonnet on the Massacre of the Christians in Bulgaria   23
Sonnet on the Sale by Auction of Keats' Love Letters   139
Sonnet to Liberty   126

Sonnet Written in Holy Week at Genoa   21
Sphinx, The   142
Sweet I blame you not for mine the fault was, had I not been made of
    common clay   106
Symphony in Yellow   141

Tædium Vitæ   126
The apple trees are hung with gold   52
The corn has turned from grey to red   5
The Gods are dead: no longer do we bring   29
The lily's withered chalice falls   132
The little white clouds are racing over the sky   40
The oleander on the wall   4
The sea is flecked with bars of grey   130
The sea was sapphire coloured, and the sky   21
The silent room, the heavy creeping shade   127
The silver trumpets rang across the Dome   24
The sin was mine; I did not understand   140
The sky is laced with fitful red   131
The Thames nocturne of blue and gold   129
The western wind is blowing fair   127
The wild bee reels from bough to bough   105
Theatre at Argos, The   22
Theocritus: A Villanelle   51
Theoretikos   29
There is no peace beneath the noon   14
There was a time in Europe long ago   26
These are the letters which Endymion wrote   139
This English Thames is holier far than Rome   41
This mighty empire hath but feet of clay   29
This winter air is keen and cold   133
Thou knowest all:—I seek in vain   11
Θρηνωιδία   11
Thy prophecies are but a lying tale   17
To drift with every passion till my soul   132
To Milton   27
To My Wife: With a Copy of My Poems   139
To outer senses there is peace   131
To stab my youth with desperate knives, to wear   126
To that gaunt House of Art which lacks for naught   87
Tread lightly, she is near   3
True Knowledge, The   11
Two crownèd Kings, and One that stood alone   20

Under the Balcony   138
Under the rose-tree's dancing shade   136
Urbs Sacra Æterna   22

Vision, A   20
Vita Nuova   25

Was this His coming! I had hoped to see   27
Wasted Days   28
We caught the tread of dancing feet   134
Where hast thou been since round the walls of Troy   89
With a Copy of 'A House of Pomegranates'   141
Within this restless, hurried, modern world   106

A SELECTION OF   **OXFORD WORLD'S CLASSICS**

JANE AUSTEN   **Catharine and Other Writings**
                      Emma
                      Mansfield Park
                      Northanger Abbey, Lady Susan, The
                          Watsons, and **Sanditon**
                      Persuasion
                      Pride and Prejudice
                      Sense and Sensibility

ANNE BRONTË   **Agnes Grey**
                      The Tenant of Wildfell Hall

CHARLOTTE BRONTË   **Jane Eyre**
                      The Professor
                      Shirley
                      Villette

EMILY BRONTË   **Wuthering Heights**

WILKIE COLLINS   **The Moonstone**
                      No Name
                      The Woman in White

CHARLES DARWIN   **The Origin of Species**

CHARLES DICKENS   **The Adventures of Oliver Twist**
                      Bleak House
                      David Copperfield
                      Great Expectations
                      Hard Times
                      Little Dorrit
                      Martin Chuzzlewit
                      Nicholas Nickleby
                      The Old Curiosity Shop
                      Our Mutual Friend
                      The Pickwick Papers
                      A Tale of Two Cities

A SELECTION OF   OXFORD WORLD'S CLASSICS

GEORGE ELIOT   Adam Bede
                           Daniel Deronda
                           Middlemarch
                           The Mill on the Floss
                           Silas Marner

ELIZABETH GASKELL   Cranford
                           The Life of Charlotte Brontë
                           Mary Barton
                           North and South
                           Wives and Daughters

THOMAS HARDY   Far from the Madding Crowd
                           Jude the Obscure
                           The Mayor of Casterbridge
                           A Pair of Blue Eyes
                           The Return of the Native
                           Tess of the d'Urbervilles
                           The Woodlanders

WALTER SCOTT   Ivanhoe
                           Rob Roy
                           Waverley

MARY SHELLEY   Frankenstein
                           The Last Man

ROBERT LOUIS   Kidnapped and Catriona
STEVENSON   The Strange Case of Dr Jekyll and
                               Mr Hyde and Weir of Hermiston
                           Treasure Island

BRAM STOKER   Dracula

WILLIAM MAKEPEACE   Barry Lyndon
THACKERAY   Vanity Fair

OSCAR WILDE   Complete Shorter Fiction
                           The Picture of Dorian Gray

TROLLOPE IN   OXFORD WORLD'S CLASSICS

ANTHONY TROLLOPE   An Autobiography

Ayala's Angel

Barchester Towers

The Belton Estate

The Bertrams

Can You Forgive Her?

The Claverings

Cousin Henry

Doctor Thorne

Doctor Wortle's School

The Duke's Children

Early Short Stories

The Eustace Diamonds

An Eye for an Eye

Framley Parsonage

He Knew He Was Right

Lady Anna

The Last Chronicle of Barset

Later Short Stories

Miss Mackenzie

Mr Scarborough's Family

Orley Farm

Phineas Finn

Phineas Redux

The Prime Minister

Rachel Ray

The Small House at Allington

La Vendée

The Warden

The Way We Live Now

A SELECTION OF   **OXFORD WORLD'S CLASSICS**

HANS CHRISTIAN **Fairy Tales**
ANDERSEN

J. M. BARRIE **Peter Pan in Kensington Gardens** and
Peter and Wendy

L. FRANK BAUM **The Wonderful Wizard of Oz**

FRANCES HODGSON **The Secret Garden**
BURNETT

LEWIS CARROLL **Alice's Adventures in Wonderland** and
Through the Looking-Glass

CARLO COLLODI **The Adventures of Pinocchio**

KENNETH GRAHAME **The Wind in the Willows**

THOMAS HUGHES **Tom Brown's Schooldays**

CHARLES KINGSLEY **The Water-Babies**

GEORGE MACDONALD **The Princess and the Goblin** and **The
Princess and Curdie**

EDITH NESBIT **Five Children and It**
The Railway Children

ANNA SEWELL **Black Beauty**

JOHANN DAVID WYSS **The Swiss Family Robinson**

THE OXFORD SHERLOCK HOLMES

ARTHUR CONAN DOYLE   **The Adventures of Sherlock Holmes**

The Case-Book of Sherlock Holmes

His Last Bow

The Hound of the Baskervilles

The Memoirs of Sherlock Holmes

The Return of Sherlock Holmes

The Valley of Fear

Sherlock Holmes Stories

The Sign of the Four

A Study in Scarlet

A SELECTION OF   **OXFORD WORLD'S CLASSICS**

SERGEI AKSAKOV   **A Russian Gentleman**

ANTON CHEKHOV   **Early Stories**
Five Plays
The Princess and Other Stories
The Russian Master and Other Stories
The Steppe and Other Stories
Twelve Plays
Ward Number Six and Other Stories
A Woman's Kingdom and Other Stories

FYODOR DOSTOEVSKY   **An Accidental Family**
Crime and Punishment
Devils
A Gentle Creature and Other Stories
The Idiot
The Karamazov Brothers
Memoirs from the House of the Dead
Notes from the Underground and
   The Gambler

NIKOLAI GOGOL   **Village Evenings Near Dikanka** and
   Mirgorod
Plays and Petersburg

ALEXANDER HERZEN   **Childhood, Youth, and Exile**

MIKHAIL LERMONTOV   **A Hero of our Time**

ALEXANDER PUSHKIN   **Eugene Onegin**
The Queen of Spades and Other Stories

LEO TOLSTOY   **Anna Karenina**
The Kreutzer Sonata and Other Stories
The Raid and Other Stories
Resurrection
War and Peace

IVAN TURGENEV   **Fathers and Sons**
First Love and Other Stories
A Month in the Country

The Oxford World's Classics Website

www.worldsclassics.co.uk

- Information about new titles
- Explore the full range of Oxford World's Classics
- Links to other literary sites and the main OUP webpage
- Imaginative competitions, with bookish prizes
- Peruse *Compass*, the Oxford World's Classics magazine
- Articles by editors
- Extracts from Introductions
- A forum for discussion and feedback on the series
- Special information for teachers and lecturers

www.worldsclassics.co.uk

MORE ABOUT   **OXFORD WORLD'S CLASSICS**

American Literature

British and Irish Literature

Children's Literature

Classics and Ancient Literature

Colonial Literature

Eastern Literature

European Literature

History

Medieval Literature

Oxford English Drama

Poetry

Philosophy

Politics

Religion

The Oxford Shakespeare

A complete list of Oxford Paperbacks, including Oxford World's Classics, OPUS, Past Masters, Oxford Authors, Oxford Shakespeare, Oxford Drama, and Oxford Paperback Reference, is available in the UK from the Academic Division Publicity Department, Oxford University Press, Great Clarendon Street, Oxford OX2 6DP.

In the USA, complete lists are available from the Paperbacks Marketing Manager, Oxford University Press, 198 Madison Avenue, New York, NY 10016.

Oxford Paperbacks are available from all good bookshops. In case of difficulty, customers in the UK can order direct from Oxford University Press Bookshop, Freepost, 116 High Street, Oxford OX1 4BR, enclosing full payment. Please add 10 per cent of published price for postage and packing.